Revelations about Revelation

An Explanation of the Apocalypse of John for the Layman

Larry G. Pittman

ISBN 979-8-89112-235-2 (Paperback)
ISBN 979-8-89112-236-9 (Digital)

Covenant Books
Meadville, PA
www.covenantbooks.com

Contents

Preface..v

Chapter 1: Some Preliminary Questions 1

Chapter 2: A Vision for the Church (Revelation 1:1–20)............7

Chapter 3: No Middle Ground (Revelation 2:1–3:22) 15

Chapter 4: Round the Throne of God (Revelation 4:1–5:14).....30

Chapter 5: A Vision of the Faithful (Revelation 6:1–8:5) 37

Chapter 6: The Undoing of the Creation
(Revelation 8:6–9:21)..44

Chapter 7: Whose Kingdom Is This? (Revelation 10:1–11:19)...51

Chapter 8: The Adversary (Revelation 12:1–17) 58

Chapter 9: In the Image of Satan (Revelation 13:1–18) 66

Chapter 10: A Call to Endurance (Revelation 14:1–20) 75

Chapter 11: The Wrath of God (Revelation 15:1–16:21).............82

Chapter 12: The Mother of Harlots and the Beast
(Revelation 17:1–18)..90

Chapter 13: The Victory of Righteousness
(Revelation 18:1–19:21)..97

Chapter 14: The Final Judgment (Revelation 20:1–15) 104

Chapter 15: The New Jerusalem (Revelation 21:1–27) 114

Chapter 16: Back to the Garden (Revelation 22:1–21)..............121

Chapter 17: "What About the Antichrist?" 129

Bibliography..135

Endnotes..137

Preface

I was ordained to the Gospel ministry on March 20, 1983, and had a couple years of pastoral experience as a student and candidate for ordination prior to that. Ever since I have been engaged in pastoral ministry, I have found that some laypeople are hesitant even to read the Apocalypse of John because it has so thoroughly confused them when they have tried to read it. Some, having heard or read at least a portion of the teachings of Hal Lindsey and other such interpreters of Scripture, are actually afraid to read the final book of the New Testament because, based on the erroneous teachings of such folks, they find the images in the Apocalypse to be frightening and unthinkable predictions concerning our present day and the near future. Most people in our time are simply not equipped to understand this portion of Scripture without some help.

It occurred to me that this problem was too widespread for me to hope to make a difference in the situation through my local preaching and teaching in the particular congregation that I served. I felt an urgent sense of the Holy Spirit leading me to write this book to do more about that.

I consider myself to be what I would call a "layman's Pastor." By that I mean that in spite of my education and ordination as a Presbyterian Minister of the Word and Sacraments, I am still a layman at heart and have not forgotten or surrendered the perspective I had as a layman. I remember what it was like to have concerns my pastor didn't seem to share and to be filled with an awareness that there were things I did not understand as a layman, the knowledge of which the pastor seemed to take for granted. I remember that as a layman, I sensed an unnatural gap between myself and the clergy. I want to help close that gap for others by sharing knowledge I have gained, rather than keeping it to myself as a badge of superiority as some clergy seem to do. As a Protestant, I do not consider ordained clergy to be of any higher order than the laity. While we are called to a special type of service to the Lord and His people, we are not in any way superior to the laity. That is why anything that seems to suggest that we are strikes me as unnatural, according to the Lord's scheme of things.

There are things which most laypeople do not know or comprehend about the Bible, simply because they have not had the opportunity of experiencing the kind of intensive study of the Bible in terms of its context and production that is available in seminary training, of which the responsible minister should avail himself or herself. This makes it inevitable that most laypeople (and many ministers who are less than responsible in the area of biblical scholarship) are vastly ignorant when it comes to the true nature of much of the Scriptures. This can result in a tendency to take literally even those portions of Scripture in which the language and form are highly symbolic, and even to miss out on much of the meaning of those portions which were intended to be taken literally.

When a portion of Scripture is intended to be symbolic, there is no way to understand it accurately by taking it literally. It just doesn't make sense. Of course, in Hal Lindsey's case, he seems to recognize that the Apocalypse of John is written in symbolic language, but he fails to take seriously enough the context and meaning of the book for the time in which it was written. Thus, he is too quick to assume that the Book of Revelation speaks of the twentieth century or beyond. At any rate, most laypeople and many ministers do not have the necessary background knowledge (or do not apply that knowledge) to understand what in the world John is talking about in Revelation.

This does not mean that they are stupid or that they cannot receive any benefit from reading God's Word. It is just that in the very special case of the Apocalypse of John, there is too much symbolism for anyone of our time to understand the book properly without having that symbolism explained to them with proper attention to its context. Providing an explanation of that context is what I want to do in this book.

Some might ask why this is important enough for me to devote my time to it. As a Minister of the Word and Sacraments, I am keenly aware of the responsibility to which God calls the Pastor to assist God's people in gaining access to His Word so that it may have its full intended impact upon and through their lives. I am convinced that even though anyone who is seeking God's will can simply read the Bible and gain from that reading sufficient understanding for salvation and guidance, we are called to growth in the Spirit, which necessitates an ever-deepening immersion in God's Word and a greater maturity in our understanding of it. I am further convinced that the fullest possible understanding of the rest of the New Testament cannot be had without unlocking the mysteries of the Apocalypse of John. I offer this book of explanation in order to enhance the understanding of God's Word by His people, and in terms I hope will be plain and simple enough to be accessible to anyone, regardless of their level of previous biblical study. I hope that my efforts here may enhance devotion to Christ and commitment to serve Him by lifting the veil that has kept many from the full blessing of reading the last book of the Bible and offering a clearer view through John's vision.

This book is not intended to be a technical piece. It is not written for professors, but to assist the understanding of the average layperson trying to make sense out of the strange images of the Apocalypse of John. My work arises from a deep concern in response to a lot of irresponsible teaching by certain literalistic fundamentalists who try to see the twentieth century or beyond in John's prophecy and in the process do much violence to the biblical text and to the reader's ability to gain an accurate understanding of it.

There will be few footnotes and not much bibliography because I shall be quoting few particular sources. I am not attempting to produce the kind of grand scholarly work one might expect if I were a college or seminary professor. I am not trying to rehash what so many others have already said. To my knowledge, much of what I have to say, no one has said before. The knowledge I seek to share in this work is the cumulative result of my study of the book of

Revelation under my professors in college and seminary, and most particularly under Dr. C. Frank Jacks, with whom I studied in a tutorial relationship for over a year. I have consulted *The Layman's Bible Commentary* and *The Communicator's Commentary* on Revelation to jog my memory in explaining basic symbolism in the book, but I have reached some conclusions of my own which are not clearly traceable to anything I have read. It would be almost impossible to make accurate references to specific writers by way of footnotes or bibliography because what I am sharing here is the result of my own studies and careful thought about the text itself, in its own context, and not a restatement of the commentaries of others. I am sharing the cake, not the recipe, so to speak. Any quotations from Scripture are taken either from the Revised Standard Version or the English Standard Version unless otherwise noted.

Readers may wish to consult those commentaries mentioned above, and other works, such as Hal Lindsey's *The Late Great Planet Earth* or Billy Graham's *Approaching Hoofbeats*, for comparison. I do not claim to have all the answers or to possess perfect knowledge. However, I do feel that I am putting forward in this book some original ideas about the Apocalypse of John which merit some consideration. I hope that my efforts herein will accomplish my purpose of making this marvelous last book of the New Testament more accessible to the average man or woman in the pew. After all, I am not writing for advanced scholars, but to assist the understanding of the ordinary layperson, as I believe any Pastor ought to try to do. I offer my own interpretation of the Book of Revelation with the hope that it will provoke others to careful thought about what John has written, and will help the readers see its importance for their own living in Christ. You, the reader, will note that I do not worry about some of the usual formalities, such as writing everything in the third person. Rather, my approach as I write is as if I were sitting in the home of a church member, or in my office, informally chatting with him or her about the Apocalypse. I hope and pray my work will come across that way and have that kind of effect.

CHAPTER I

Some Preliminary Questions

A. What Is an Apocalypse?

The word "apocalypse" means revelation, in the sense of taking something out of hiding. It means making something known that has previously been kept hidden. It is a word formed in English by taking the Greek word and writing it in its equivalent English letters. This is called "transliteration."

Whenever we speak of God revealing Himself or something else to us, it is to be understood that He is taking something that has been "hidden" from our understanding or knowledge and making it known to us. He is introducing us to something we could not have known otherwise and offering us inside knowledge of His opinion and will concerning the matter He is revealing and our relationship to it.

In this general sense, the whole Bible might be thought of as apocalypse or revelation. However, in a more technical and specific sense, the word "apocalypse," and its adjectival form, "apocalyptic," refer to a highly symbolic form of literature represented by a number of writings the Jews produced during times in which they were dominated by other nations, especially during the time between the writing of the Old Testament books and the writing of the New Testament books. Such literature was written to encourage the people to remain faithful to God and resist their oppressors. It served as a call to arms in support of those who rose up to drive out the oppressors and regain freedom for the Jews. Because this literature could prove dangerous to the writers and recipients if it fell into the wrong hands, it was deliberately written in symbolic language that would not be understood by the enemy.

One example, actually included in the Old Testament, is the Book of Daniel, written in support of the Maccabean Wars against the Syrian oppressors in the second century BC. To keep the Syrian overlords from understanding it, that book was written in the guise of a historical narrative concerning a fictitious prophet named Daniel, supposedly living in the time of the Babylonian Exile, four hundred years earlier. The Babylonian Exile was used as a symbolic reference to the time of Syrian oppression the people were facing at the time Daniel was written. The story of Daniel's faithfulness to God was a call to the people to remain faithful in their present struggle. The "abomination that makes desolate" in Daniel 11:31 refers to a pagan altar set up on the altar of the Temple in Jerusalem, upon which a pig was sacrificed by order of the Syrian emperor Antiochus IV, thus defiling the temple of God so that it could not be used for Jewish worship until it was later cleansed and rededicated.

The Syrians would not understand this symbolic literature, and probably did not put forth the effort to suppress it as they would have done if it had been written in literal terms, speaking plainly about the current events with which it was really concerned. The Jews, however, understood what the writer was really talking about and were strengthened by the Book of Daniel to keep on fighting.

What Daniel was to the Jews of the second century BC, the Apocalypse of John was to Christians at the time it was written. In both cases, since the writing is apocalyptic, it must not be taken literally, because it was not intended to be. In order to understand Revelation properly, it is necessary to learn the meaning of its symbolism. First, however, it is also necessary to consider who wrote the Apocalypse, to whom it was written and why, and when it was written.

B. Who Wrote the Apocalypse of John?

The writer of the Book of Revelation claims to be John, a servant of God, "who bore witness to the word of God and to the testimony of Jesus Christ." It must be admitted immediately that this does not give us a positive identification of the author, so we need to try to figure out who it was. After all, if you receive a letter from someone, it will make more sense if you know who that someone is.

Tradition has it that this book was written by one of Jesus' twelve Apostles, John, the son of Zebedee. The present work assumes this to be the case. However, there are those who argue against John's authorship, and it would be irresponsible not to answer some of their arguments.

One argument against John's authorship is that the wording and style of writing in the Apocalypse are very different from what we find in the Gospel According to John. So it is argued by some who accept John the Apostle as the author of the Fourth Gospel that the Apocalypse could not have been written by the same man. The same folks doubt that the writer of the Apocalypse could be the same as the author of the three Letters of John. Some say these five books could not all have been authored by John the Apostle, or by any other one person, because the gospel and the three letters attributed to John show a greater command of the Greek language than does the Apocalypse. Some even say John could have written the Apocalypse, but not the other works, because he would not have had this command of Greek. Of course, there are those who deny that John the Apostle wrote any of these books.

These objections to John's authorship have no merit, really. Nothing could be simpler to answer. If John, an uneducated fisherman, could not have mastered the Greek language sufficiently to write the gospel and the three letters that bear his name, then he would naturally have gotten a friend who had such mastery to write for him, putting into good koine Greek (the common people's Greek) the ideas and information John wished to convey. Paul clearly had friends, such as Tertius (see Romans 16:22), who wrote for him as he dictated his letters to the churches. Why could not John have done the same thing? At any rate, the testimony of Polycarp that John is the author of the Gospel of John should be taken as sufficient evidence, since Polycarp knew John personally.

As for those who say that John could not be the author of the gospel and the letters on the one hand, and also of the Apocalypse on the other, it seems that they have paid too little attention to Revelation 1:9, where John tells us he was "on the isle of Patmos on account of the word of God and the testimony of Jesus," in the same sentence in which he speaks of sharing in the "tribulation and the kingdom, and the patient endurance" of a faithful and persecuted Church. Clearly, John was exiled to Patmos as a punishment for his witness for Christ, received the vision of the Apocalypse there, and most likely committed it to writing while still there. The reason the Greek is not as good in the Apocalypse as it is in the gospel and the letters must be that when John was on Patmos, in exile, either a different helper with a lesser command of Greek wrote for him, or else no such helper was available, and John had to do the writing himself. It is entirely feasible that John had learned enough Greek to accomplish this, even if he did not know the language well enough to compose the gospel and the letters, as well as they were written, without help.

As for the claim that the letters of John were written by some other person named John, who was called "the Elder," this is another example of the tendency some have of making things complicated that are really quite simple. The Greek word for "elder," referring to an officer of the Church, basically means "old man." If John lived as late into the last decade of the first century as tradition claims, he would have been a very old man, indeed. In addition, the titles for officers in the Church were not as rigidly fixed in those days as they are today. The man whom we remember as John the Apostle might very appropriately have referred to himself as an Elder, as the author does in the greetings of II John and III John. (See also I Peter 5:1.) There is no reason to assume that John the Elder was not, or could not have been, the same as John the Apostle.[1]

Another objection is that the subject matter and style of the Apocalypse differ so much from the gospel and the letters that they could not have come from the same author. This argument simply does not hold water. Of course the style is different! The Apocalypse is a dramatically different type of literature. That doesn't mean it could not have been authored by the same person from whom we have received the other Johannine books. The style of any apocalyptic writing would be unavoidably different from a personal letter or documentary account, even if all three were written by the same person on the same day. Apocalyptic literature is, by nature and definition, very different. As for different subject matter, since when can one person not write about various concerns? Just read through the works of C. S. Lewis. There is a great difference between *The Chronicles of Narnia* and *Mere Christianity.* Also, I intend to show that there is at least one connecting thread between the Gospel According to John and the Revelation of John. It has to do with a passage from Zechariah 12:10–11. The relevance of this passage to the Gospel According to John and The Revelation of John and their relationship to each other is too significant to be coincidental. Also, the references to this passage in both books bear positions too strategic and too important in each of them to be merely incidental to the message the writer seeks to convey. This will be brought out more clearly later.

In summation, there is simply no real evidence to overthrow tradition and the finding of the vast majority of the early "Fathers" of the Church that John authored all five books attributed to him. The burden of proof is upon those who doubt it.

C. To Whom Was the Apocalypse Addressed, and Why?

In Revelation 1:4, John addresses himself to "the seven churches that are in Asia." In Revelation 1:11, he is instructed to "Write what you see in a book and send it to the seven churches, to Ephesus and to Smyrna and to Pergamum and to Thyatira and to Sardis and to Philadelphia and to Laodicea." These seven cities were the major cities of the Roman province of Asia, also known as Asia Minor, or what is now modern Turkey. So it was to Christians in that part of the Roman Empire that John specifically addressed the Apocalypse.

As the text makes clear, he was writing to them to give them encouragement and instruction as they faced a time of severe persecution. These matters will be further emphasized and clarified as we deal with the text itself. It needs to be noted at this point, however, that the fact that John was writing specifically to Christians in the Roman province of Asia does not mean that Revelation has no relevance for Christians today. It simply means he was thinking about them and their needs at that time, not about us or our time.

D. When Was the Apocalypse Written?

The question of the date of the writing of the Apocalypse is inseparable from the questions of authorship and occasion already mentioned. Most scholars would place the date of this writing within the time frame of one or the other of two periods of Roman persecution against Christians in the first century AD. One of these was the persecution under Nero. The other was the persecution under Domitian. Since the Apocalypse is clearly addressed to the Asian church and the campaign of persecution which directly affected them was under Domitian, not Nero, it seems clear enough that it was during Domitian's persecution that John wrote. After all, he was not, as some assume, so much predicting future events as he was giving practical guidance for facing an all-too-present crisis. This would place the date of the Apocalypse somewhere during the reign of Domitian, 81–96 AD, probably after 90 AD. This will be further clarified in dealing with the text itself.

Chapter 2

A Vision for the Church
(Revelation 1:1–20)

Proverbs 29:18 declares, "Where there is no vision, the people perish." A true prophet of God was one who received a vision, or visions, from God to be shared with His people, and proclaimed the truth thus revealed to him for a warning or encouragement or instruction to God's people.

There was not a true prophet of God among the Jews for about five hundred years, until John the Baptizer arose as the forerunner of Jesus of Nazareth. Beginning with the Baptizer, continuing through the ministry of Jesus, and on through the first several decades of Christianity, prophecy was restored. Scattered throughout the early Church, there were people who were given the special gift of prophecy. John the Apostle was one of these people. The Revelation of John is an account given by John, the son of Zebedee, one of the Lord's twelve Apostles, of a lengthy vision which was given to him as a vision for the Church. He shares this vision with the Church so that the people of God might not perish.

John presents his account of this vision in the form of an encyclical. The seven churches which are named in Revelation 1:11, and to which the seven letters in chapters two and three are addressed, are the seven major churches, located in the seven major cities of the Roman province of Asia. John intends this writing to be circulated among these churches and to be shared eventually with the whole Church in the province of Asia. He is not writing just to these seven individual congregations, although there is good reason for addressing what he has to say primarily to them. More on that will be presented later.

The number 7 is the symbol for wholeness, completeness, and perfection. So when John addresses his writing to "the seven churches that are in Asia," it is not meant to exclude any smaller churches which may exist in that province, but includes every Christian in every congregation in Asia, represented by these seven.

In the first eight verses, John makes it clear that he is writing to convey a message from Christ Himself. The greeting in verses 4 and 5 is not a greeting from John, but from the Triune God. The Holy Spirit is referred to here as "the seven spirits who are before His throne." This is not to say there are literally seven Holy Spirits, but rather John speaks symbolically of the perfection and wholeness of God, which the number "7" represents, and the fact that the Holy Spirit is present to the seven churches addressed. John wants his readers to understand this message is not from him alone, but from Him who is "the firstborn of the dead, and the ruler of kings upon earth." He is writing to encourage and exhort the gentile Christians in Asia to remain faithful and endure with patience the persecution they face, which is getting worse. He reminds them that their hope is in Him who is "coming with the clouds." In apocalyptic writings, clouds are the standard symbol of God's judgment. John is saying that the Vindicator and Deliverer of these people who suffer is the Christ who will come again to judge the inhabitants of the whole earth.

John both warns and encourages these people to be faithful in the midst of their troubles because they are servants of Jesus who is "the Alpha and the Omega"—the first and the last—"the Lord God, who is and who was and who is to come." John wants to urge them to be firm in their faith as he is in Him who "was in the beginning with God," who "became flesh and dwelt among us," and who promised to "come again and to take you to myself" (John 1:2, 14; 14:3).

John delivers this message as one who knows firsthand what it is to be persecuted for his faith in Jesus Christ. He was driven out of Judea by other Jews who did not accept Jesus. Apparently, he has also been persecuted by unbelieving gentiles because of his faith. In Revelation 1:9, he is not saying that he is on the isle of Patmos voluntarily in order that he might bear testimony to his faith in Jesus, but rather that the Romans have exiled him there because he *has* witnessed for Jesus. He clearly connects his being on Patmos with the statement that he is sharing with his readers "the tribulation and the kingdom and the patient endurance." Contrary to some modern interpreters of Scripture, John is not talking about some "great tribulation" that is yet to come upon the world. Rather, he is talking specifically about the tribulation the Church was facing even as he wrote, which he himself was then experiencing.

Persecution was coming upon the Asian Christians, just as it had come upon Jewish Christians in Judea at the hands of unbelieving Jews, and just as it had come upon Christians in Rome at the hand of Nero. It had already begun, and he was giving them God's perspective on it and telling them how to face it as it got worse. Their pagan neighbors who were loyal to Rome, in addition to the Diaspora Jews who had run expatriated Christian Jews out of the synagogues, had already made life difficult for them by ostracizing them. Now that persecution would intensify to a matter of life and death. When John says in verse 10 that he heard "a loud voice like a trumpet," this is a military image. The sound of a trumpet is a call to battle. The Lord of the armies of Heaven is sounding the alert to His people, the Church, and calling them to stand firm in the spiritual warfare that is upon them.

Beyond the warning of troubles to come, John sought to comfort the Asian Christians with the greater message that the troubles which the Church would suffer at the hands of pagans and unbelieving Jews (which he calls the "synagogue of Satan") are nothing compared to the trouble which God will bring upon Satan and his servants who make war on the Church. John writes to assure the Church in Asia that God's judgment will come on the Roman Empire and on those who join in persecuting Christians out of allegiance to Rome. He tells them the time will be short, that God will not long allow His saints to be persecuted before He destroys Satan and his kingdom and establishes a new order in which the servants of God will see Him in His glory and live in peace with Him eternally.

In light of this assurance, John urges the Christians in Asia to be faithful even unto death and to trust in God through Jesus Christ no matter what they must suffer because the ultimate victory belongs to Christ and to His faithful ones. The victory of Christ is to be shared with those who remain faithful to Him by patiently enduring the tribulation by which Satan seeks to coerce them to deny Christ.

When John says, "I was in the Spirit on the Lord's day," he is claiming that, like the Old Testament prophets, he went into a trance by the power of the Holy Spirit and received in a vision what he is about to share with his readers. He is commanded in the vision to write down what he is about to see in order that he might share it with the Church. A vision was a special type of dream God gave to certain prophets to reveal what His people needed to know. It will be important throughout the study of John's Apocalypse to remember that all that he is telling us is a symbolic dream, which has hidden meaning and is not to be taken as a literal account or prediction of actual events.

Thus John received this vision for the Church. It was a vision with a very specific message for the Church in Asia at the end of the first century AD. It was not a prediction of some of the things in the twentieth century or beyond that many people in recent times have tried to say it is. Yet, the message of this vision is applicable to any age. The vision God gave to us through John's experience offers a vision for the Church to keep before us in times of trouble especially, but also in times that are seemingly peaceful. The temptation to lose faith can, after all, be even greater and harder to resist when things are going well for us because it is during those times that we are often least aware of our need for a strong faith in Christ.

Therefore, the very first image that is given to us in the vision is that of the glorified Christ. This is one of the most important images, perhaps the most important, in the vision. It is given at the beginning of the vision, and is meant to be kept in mind throughout. This image of Christ is the foundation on which John builds his call for the patient endurance to which he exhorts the Church. This image is in itself a vision which the Church needs to keep fresh in our collective memory and clear before our mind's eye at all times, in both good and evil days. This vision of Jesus is full of very important images, with symbolic, rather than literal meanings, that the Church always needs to understand about Christ.

Upon turning to see who had been speaking to him, John sees seven golden lamp stands and "one like a son of man" who stands in the midst of them. It is, of course, Jesus the Messiah whom John sees. Of all the terms which various Jewish writers had used to speak of the coming Messiah, "Son of Man" is the one which Jesus in His earthly ministry used most often to refer to Himself. It means that Jesus is a man—a real, flesh-and-blood human male. Jesus' own insistence upon applying this term to Himself was a profound expression of His humility in emptying Himself of His divine glory for our sake, identi-fying with us in our condition, and taking upon Himself the form of a slave to die on the cross for our sin, as Paul describes in Philippians 2:5–8. It means that instead of lording it over us that He is the Son of God, during His earthly ministry and even in His present exalta-tion at the right hand of the Father, Jesus expresses His love for us by being what we are. He is thus always capable of knowing and sharing all the same pain and fear or joy and triumph that are ours. By this, we know that He does not keep Himself aloof from us and above our troubles, but shares with us the tribulation and the Kingdom and the patient endurance, even as John claims to do for the sake of Christ. So the call to faithfulness is a call to walk deliberately with Him who walks unseen among us, for the seven lamp stands represent the seven churches, and by extension the whole Church, and the Son of Man is in the midst.

The next thing we need to notice is that the Son of Man is "clothed with a long robe and with a golden girdle round his breast." The long robe is the symbol of royalty. It signifies that Jesus is indeed the King, whose authority is supreme over all authorities in creation. It is patterned after the robe Isaiah sees God wearing in his vision in the Temple in Isaiah 6. As John has said earlier, Jesus is the "ruler of kings on earth." All governments, even those which do not acknowl-edge Him, are subject to His authority and accountable to Him. Whether Christian or atheist, just or oppressive, all who govern will answer to Him in the final judgment for how they govern. Their authority to govern rightly comes from God alone. Any abuse, mis-handling, or corruption of that authority is rebellion against Him who is King of kings and Lord of lords.

Not only is Christ supreme over all political authority, He is the supreme authority in religious matters, as well. The girdle around His waist corresponds to that worn by the Temple priests. He is, as the writer of Hebrews says, the Great High Priest of the eternal priesthood. Thus, all the false worshipers who worship the emperor and who trouble the Christians because they refuse to do so will answer to Christ for their abominations. There can be no true wor-ship which does not acknowledge Jesus Christ as the Great High Priest and also as the embodied presence of God Himself, the King over all creation.

The white hair is the symbol of the wisdom of age. He is the Ancient of Days (Daniel 7:9, 13, 22) and wiser than all of man-kind. Those who seek true and godly wisdom must come to Him to receive it as His gift. He is the source of all true wisdom, being the very Word of God incarnate. Along with His supreme wisdom goes His unequalled judgment of the hearts of men. This is symbolized by the flaming eyes, which pierce right through us and see all that is to be known within us, no matter how well we think we can keep it hidden.

That His feet are like "burnished bronze" is a symbol of His triumph over all His enemies. He has even conquered death itself: so there is none who can stand against Him. John is sharing this vision with people who are surrounded by the hatred of their own country-men and in danger of the fury of a crazed Roman emperor named Domitian, who thinks he is the incarnation of Zeus. Their enemies are many and powerful, but John is telling them that they should not fear their enemies because their enemies are first of all the enemies of Christ, and no enemy of Christ can ultimately endure or prevail. Even though they might die for their faith, those who stand firm in the Lord will finally share in the victory which He has already won over death and over every force of evil.

That His voice is like the sound of many waters means that He is unlimited in the ways that He can make His will known, and that He proclaims His will through the varied rush of human events. As He overrules the affairs of nations, even those actions which are done in defiance of His will are ultimately turned to accomplish His purpose. This is therefore a symbol of the power of His word, and of His decrees, as there is great power in the rushing of many waters. It symbolizes the life-giving and purifying power of His Word. Clear rushing water is symbolic of the Holy Spirit, whom Jesus promises to all who entrust themselves to Him. It is by the living water of the Holy Spirit that He makes His Word effective in our lives.

The sharp two-edged sword which proceeds from His mouth is a symbol of His judgment. It is the Word of God, by which all men are to be judged. Jesus is the Righteous Judge, who will decide the fate of all mankind according to the Word of God, of which He is Himself the eternal incarnation. As He is perfectly obedient to the Word of God the Father Almighty, He is Himself the standard by which all others will be judged. His face shines with the pure glory of the Holy God. It is because He is holy that He has the authority and the right to judge sinners. All who reject His Lordship will be consumed in the brilliance of His face. All who accept and proclaim His Lordship will walk in the light of His glory.

As horrifying as this awesome appearance may be to the servants of Satan, who oppose Christ and seek to destroy His Church, what a glorious truth is symbolized by the seven stars He holds in His right hand! The seven stars are the Pastors of the seven churches. That He holds them in His right hand is a sign of His favor and that He upholds them by His power and truth and righteousness. It is with this same right hand that He reaches out to John to comfort and uplift him. John has fallen senseless at Jesus' feet, unable to bear the sight of Christ's glory. He had seen this glory on the Mount of Transfiguration as he records in his gospel. Here, it overwhelms him. Christ extends His grace and compassion and power by which He upholds the Pastors of the seven churches and, by the same token, the whole church. The word "angel" really means "messenger." The pastor of a church is meant to be God's messenger to that church. The symbolism here is that so long as God's messengers are faithful, the Almighty Christ, who has all wisdom and power and glory and majesty and truth and holiness and judgment, upholds them and preserves them. Through such faithful messengers, the Church receives the true Word of God. When the Church is faithful to the Word, it is upheld and preserved by His grace and power.

This vision of Christ is for the Church today as well as yesterday, and for all ages. We should meditate on it often. It reminds us just who Christ is. While it fills us with awe, it is yet a vision that offers us great comfort as it shows us what a great and powerful, triumphant and wise, glorious and gracious Lord He is who walks silently and unseen among us, and yet speaks with so many voices. It is a vision to make us bow down humbly before Jesus, but in the light of which we no longer tremble in fear before any power on earth or in hell. It is a vision which makes even the poorest and most bitterly oppressed of God's people more truly alive and free and secure than the mightiest earthly king has ever been.

Chapter 3

No Middle Ground
(Revelation 2:1–3:22)

In the first chapter of Revelation, John presents a vision of Jesus which is meant to inspire unwavering faith—confident, obedient faith—in Jesus as the eternal Christ who overcomes all evil, rules over the affairs of men and nations, and is always in the midst of His Church to guide, comfort, and strengthen us as we struggle through this world in the hope of a better world to come. Now, in chapters 2 and 3, He turns to the task of calling the Church to account concerning its faithfulness to Him who is always faithful.

This part of the message which has come to John in a vision is presented in the form of "letters" to the seven churches in the major cities of Asia. They deal with the particular situation of each of those churches, yet bear an important message for the whole Church, as well. Although each is addressed to a particular church, every "letter" needs to be heeded by each and every church. Each "letter" addresses potential problems any church may face, and which many churches eventually do face at one time or another.

Each of these seven "letters" follows a common pattern. In each one, a particular aspect of that church's situation is pointed out to demonstrate that Christ is aware of what is going on there. Then something good about each church is pointed out for special commendation. However, there is also condemnation for some breach of faithfulness in each church, accompanied by a call to repentance, and a reference to the rewards of faithfulness. There are, however, three noteworthy exceptions to this basic pattern. Two of the churches, Smyrna and Philadelphia, receive no word of condemnation, while one church, Laodicea, is not commended. One factor which does occur in every "letter," however, is that one of the images used to describe Jesus in chapter 1 is applied to each church's situation. This is meant to show that whatever their particular sin or difficulty, the Christ whose glory is revealed in the vision of chapter 1 stands ready, willing, and able to deal with it. The churches should learn this, and depend upon Him in all circumstances. I will clarify this by pointing out which image is used to address each church as we look at each of the "letters."

Taken together, these seven "letters" tell us that in the totality of the Church, there is a constantly fluctuating mixture of faithfulness and inconstancy, triumph and turmoil, activity and neglect, sound doctrine and heresy in the life of the Church, and that every congregation needs to be alert to its own current situation so as to enhance what is good and correct what is wrong. If a church fails to do this, Christ will not uphold it; but if a church is faithful to continue the struggle to do His will, Christ will share with them the victory He has won, and sustain them in the day of trouble.

The churches in Asia were having to deal on varying levels with several critical issues. One was the matter of true or false doctrine. This was particularly critical here because of the larger issue of how to respond to the persecution to which the Apocalypse as a whole is addressed. False doctrine contributes to a weak witness. Only a firm foundation in sound doctrine, based on genuine faith, can prepare the Lord's people to present a strong witness in the face of persecution.

The seven cities in which these particular churches were located were the major cities of the province of Asia. Unlike modern cities, which care little or nothing for religious matters, these seven cities were virtually in competition to outdo one another in their worship of the Roman emperor. Each city took great pride in building an elaborate temple in which to conduct this worship. For instance, the words addressed to the Pastor of the church in Pergamum, "I know where you dwell, where Satan's throne is," refer to these temples of the emperor cult. The temple at Pergamum was the first one to be built. Since John is writing to encourage the Asian Christians to stand firm against the emperor cult, it is important for him to warn them about false doctrine within the Church. If false doctrine is not clearly rejected within the Church, the people's understanding of the true Christian Faith will not be adequate to keep them from the error of compromise with the evil around them. The specific evil which John had in mind here was the emperor cult, in which the Roman Emperor was worshiped as a god.

John specifically attacks two heresies that had arisen within the Asian churches, both of which encouraged compromise with the emperor cult. One heresy was that Christians could pretend to worship the emperor, doing all the things which the cult required, so long as in their Christian worship services, they worshiped only the true God in the name of Jesus Christ. The other was the idea that there is no longer any need for the Law of God, since we are under the grace of Christ. In other words, as long as we believe in Jesus, our conduct doesn't matter. In answer to these heresies, John insists that there is no middle ground. There is no room for compromise between allegiance to Jesus Christ and the practice of any other religion. Furthermore, He has given us a standard of right and wrong, which we are not to abandon in order to get along with the world.

John is not writing a merely theoretical paper here. He is writing to give practical guidance to Christian people who are caught in an all-too-real life-and-death dilemma. It was customary in Asia to worship one's king as a god. Being under Roman domination, these people had insisted upon worshipping the emperor as they would have done their own king. To his credit, Caesar Augustus did not allow the practice to invade Rome, other than having the late Julius Caesar declared a god. However, he did allow the Asians to worship him in their land, in accordance with the usual Roman policy of respecting the religious traditions of conquered nations. He granted the Jews in Asia an exemption from this practice, respecting their refusal to worship any but the one true and living God. It was only after Augustus died that the Roman Senate declared him a god. It became customary that each emperor would be declared divine at his death. This arrangement was accepted and agreeable to Rome and the Asians.

The trouble began when some of the emperors who came after Augustus began to take it seriously. What good was it, after all, to become a god after death? Some of the emperors chose not to wait that long. Gaius Caligula was the first of these. Nero, also, required everyone to acknowledge him as a god. His persecution of the Christians in Rome, including falsely accusing them of the burning of Rome, was largely due to their refusal to worship him.

The situation became far worse under Domitian, a madman who ruled the Roman Empire from about 81 AD to 96 AD. In the last half of his reign, Domitian decided that he was the incarnation of Zeus, father of the Greco-Roman gods. He required, as a test of loyalty, that everyone acknowledge him as "Dominvs et Devs," that is, "Lord and God." This immediately put both Jews and Christians at odds with the emperor. The Jews would call no man by these titles, and the only man to whom Christians should attribute them is Jesus.

The Christians in Asia had already suffered mild persecution from their pagan Asian countrymen because they refused to worship the emperor. Now they were also persecuted by the Roman state because they refused to recognize the divinity of Domitian. Jews and, therefore, Jewish Christians, of course, were exempt, as I have already explained. But no gentile Christians had this exemption. So they were fair game for the ensuing orgy of torture and execution that arose against their refusal to call Domitian "Lord and God."

John is addressing the fact that these Christians must make a choice. Either they could worship Christ exclusively and risk the loss of business or of the rights of citizenship and even possibly risk torture and death, or they could, in addition to their Christian worship, join in the rituals of the emperor cult for the sake of appearance, and thus be spared any tribulation. Some in the Church were advising the people to take the latter course, pretending to worship Domitian as well as Jesus. John wrote the Apocalypse to declare, "You can't do that! There is no middle ground! Either Christ alone is your Lord and God, and you declare that fact boldly before all the world, or you have no part in Him at all!" In the process of conveying this message, John deals with other matters, as well, but this is the main focus. It is all connected to this.

The church in Ephesus had been Paul's base of operations in Asia. John had also spent much of his time among the Christians there, and had developed a deep relationship with them. It was a strategically important congregation in the history of the Church. It is significant that the image from the earlier vision of Christ which John applies to their situation is that of Christ holding the pastors in the palm of His right hand and walking among the churches. This is to remind them of the Lord's sustaining power and presence. Appropriately enough, this reassuring image is followed by the statement that Jesus knows their situation, as will be the case in all seven "letters." He is powerfully present, and He is aware. They are to draw strength from the assurance that He is involved. It is reminiscent of God's words to Moses on the mountain, "I have seen the affliction of my people…and have heard their cry…I know their sufferings, and I have come down to deliver them" (Exodus 3:7–8).

As John presents this vision, Jesus commends the church at Ephesus for standing firm against falsehood without wavering. Yet He accuses them of having lost their first love. Perhaps they had gotten so caught up in defending sound doctrine against heresy that they, like the Pharisees, had lost sight of the love for sinners to which Christ calls His people. Correct doctrine is important because false doctrine will lead people straight to hell. However, if your focus on doctrine leaves no place for the love Christ would have us share, it probably isn't going to do much good for the lost. This was the problem Jesus had with the Pharisees. He certainly wouldn't want the same thing happening in His church. If this was the problem in Ephesus, it would most likely have caused them to fall away from their early zeal for evangelism in their community so that they were not maintaining their outreach to lost sinners as they had done at first. People don't have much use for our doctrine if we don't help them understand that God loves them and desires their reconciliation. Apparently, neither does Jesus.

In addition, perhaps they had fallen into the rut so many churches in our day also have of keeping up what they have been doing out of a sense of duty or mere habit, rather than maintaining the same zealous love for Christ that was their original motivation in Christian witness. Eventually, this leads to a church no longer doing the Lord's work at all. At Ephesus, it hadn't deteriorated to that point yet. They were still doing the work and countering false beliefs but perhaps had lost some of their effectiveness because they had lost the realization of their love for Christ as their focus. Love is a decision, and a relationship that must be nurtured. Jesus calls them to renew their commitment to that relationship with Him before He has to remove them, like a gardener pruning the vine. (John 15:5–6)

Still, He commends the Ephesians for their opposition to the Nicolaitans. Not much is known about the Nicolaitans, except that they seem to have been a group of antinomians.[2] "Antinomian" means "against law." These people refused to accept any rules or regulations about moral behavior. Antinomians taught that what we do with our bodies has no effect upon our "souls," and we can, therefore, indulge our fleshly desires. The idea was that the "soul" was all that mattered; so if you had saving knowledge of Jesus, you could do whatever you wanted with your body. If the Nicolaitans were indeed proponents of such distorted theology, they would not surprisingly endorse the kind of compromise with the emperor cult which John opposes and seeks to discredit.

At the end of each "letter," there is a statement making a promise to those who conquer, and an admonition to "hear what the Spirit says to the churches." Thus the point is made that the persecution these folks must suffer is a spiritual warfare, and that those who wish to triumph over the spiritual forces of evil must give heed to the voice of God's Spirit. The promise to the faithful who overcome evil at Ephesus is that they will "eat of the tree of life, which is in the paradise of God." This signifies the complete restoration of full relationship with God that was forfeited by our sin. Once again, as at the creation, God will give life that is filled with the holiness and joy of His eternal, sustaining presence. But this time, it will not end.

The image of Christ that is applied to the situation at Smyrna is the One who is at the beginning and at the end, who has died and returned to life. He does not speak of their works, but of their suffering. They are reminded that He, too, has suffered trouble and poverty and slander and imprisonment and death. He will be with them as they suffer at the hands of Satan's servants, including the "synagogue of Satan." This probably means the Jews in Smyrna who contaminated their worship with pagan elements and/or sought to convert Christians to Judaism. They took great pleasure from those Christians who failed to stand firm for Jesus under such pressure. Also, Smyrna was the leading center of emperor worship, so the pressure on Christians to conform would have been tremendous there. They are promised by the One who has Himself conquered death that, even if they die for Him, what they have to gain by faithfulness is far greater than what they have to fear. They may die in the struggle they face, but the second death, the ultimate destruction of the unrepentant, will not threaten them.

Today's Christians need to heed the fact that Jesus does not promise that we will be exempt from suffering. Most church members today are more concerned with avoiding any unpleasantness than they are with being faithful disciples. This is why those who preach the false "health and wealth gospel" are so popular. Such nominal Christians don't want a Christ who might lead them in any way which might involve suffering. Jesus declares to the church at Smyrna, and to Christians today, that because they belong to Him, the devil will indeed cause them to suffer. The reference to "ten days" of tribulation does not specify a certain length of time. Ten is a whole number, which symbolizes the fullness or entirety of a thing. Ten days of tribulation denotes a full measure of crushing trouble, but for a limited time. Yes, Satan can and will make these people suffer; but because they belong to Christ, Satan's power to afflict them will not last for long. Jesus, during His earthly ministry, had said, "Whoever would save his life will lose it; and whoever loses his life for my sake and the gospel's will save it" (Mark 8:35). Now He calls the Church to "be faithful unto death, and I will give you the crown of life." Even the threat of death must not compromise our witness and service to Him who died for us, who alone can give us life.

The image addressed to Pergamum is that of Christ with the "sharp two-edged sword" of the Word of God issuing from His mouth. This is an important image for the folks at Pergamum, because they dwell in one of the enemy's great strongholds. There has been at least one fatality by Satan's warfare against this church already. His name is Antipas. So the folks at Pergamum are right in the thick of the battle. They are commended for holding firm to the Faith, even in the face of this man's martyrdom.

Yet, there are some rotten apples, even in such a good barrel as this church. Pergamum is plagued with the Nicolaitan heresy mentioned earlier. The call to repent apparently means that the Pastor and the church have not taken steps to put away this heresy from their midst. If they do not do so, Christ Himself threatens to bring trouble within the church. He promises to rid them of the contamination by applying a good dose of His truth.

Often in a church false beliefs are allowed to go unchallenged until eventually no one seems to know the difference anymore. To cure this, Christ will sometimes raise up someone within that church who knows the truth and is willing to stand up for it. When truth and falsehood clash, it can tear a congregation apart. Christ would rather that this were not necessary, considering the trouble these folks at Pergamum have already endured and have yet to face. But as Paul wrote to the Corinthian church, "There must be factions among you in order that those who are genuine among you may be recognized" (I Corinthians 11:19). As distasteful as it may be to have disputes and controversies in a church, it is better to go ahead and get it over with, and hopefully let Christ rebuild from the ashes than to surrender the church to falsehood. If the faithful at Pergamum will repent of their apathetic tolerance of the Nicolaitans and purify their doctrine and church life, Christ promises to feed them "the hidden manna" and to give each of them "a white stone, with a new name written on the stone, which no one knows except him who receives it." The "hidden manna" refers to Christ Himself as the Bread of Heaven or the Bread of Life. (John 6:30–59) This is another way of saying that the faithful will be given life in Him. The white stone is the precious jewel or treasure of being named a child of God in Christ, a new creature. No one can know the meaning of this treasure unless they receive it themselves. That the jewel is white symbolizes both the victory and the purity Christ gives.

Thyatira is praised because, in contrast to Pergamum, they are growing more fruitful as they go along, doing greater works than they did at the first. Yet, even at Thyatira, there is a need for setting things in order. This church is plagued with a false teacher who calls herself a prophetess. The image of Christ that is applied to this church's situation is that of One with flaming eyes and bronze feet. In spite of this woman's claim to be a prophetess, Jesus sees the true condition and content of her heart and mind. He calls her "Jezebel," not because that is her name, but because she is apparently similar to the evil wife of Ahab. She seeks to lead God's people into false worship and immoral behavior. The reference to "the deep things of Satan" probably indicates that she advocated the use of witchcraft and tried to disguise her heresy as a deeper understanding of the teachings of Jesus. The Greek word, *porneia*, translated "immorality," means prostitution or other sexual misconduct. Coupled with the reference to food offered to idols, it probably refers to false worship involving ritual prostitution. Perhaps this woman was actually encouraging licentious behavior in the church, or perhaps this is a symbolic reference to idol worship, which means she was encouraging the people to compromise and worship the emperor. Whatever the specifics were, the Lord's words make it clear that this woman was a corrupting influence on some in the church at Thyatira, while claiming to speak for the Lord. The church is scolded mildly for tolerating her. There is a severe warning against her and her followers as to the great punishment they may suffer if they do not repent. The letter concludes with an indication that the Lord is otherwise well pleased with the church at Thyatira, and a promise that if the faithful will only continue their current pattern of spiritual progress and purity, they will share in the glory and reign of the Messiah, which is alluded to by several familiar messianic images from the Old Testament.

The image of Christ applied to the situation of the church at Sardis is that of One who "has the seven spirits of God and the seven stars." As discussed earlier, "seven spirits" refers to the perfection of the Holy Spirit. The Sardis church was apparently one of those churches like we so often see in our day, which just go through the motions of religion without any vital expression of the faith they profess. They have rejected the Holy Spirit, and don't even realize that they have. They are a dead church, "having a form of godliness, but denying the power thereof" (I Timothy 3:5). As is sometimes the case in such a church, there are a few faithful servants of the Lord at Sardis. The Lord assures them of their place in His Kingdom in spite of their misfortune of being stuck in such a church. Plenty of vital, active Christians in the modern Church can relate to their situation. The Lord seeks to alert the church at Sardis to their need for revival and openness to receive His Spirit. The Holy Spirit is the life breath of the Church. Like so many present-day pew sitters, most of the folks at Sardis had no idea what they were missing by being content to call themselves a church without seeking to live the life of Christ as a church should.

As the seven stars represent the seven "angels" or Pastors of the seven churches, it appears that the Lord is reprimanding the Pastor at Sardis for letting the people forget the Spirit and thus fail to live out Christ's claim upon their lives and His purpose for them. As is too often the case, a few members of the church were trying to carry the load intended for the whole church. It just can't be done. So they needed their Pastor to challenge the complacent ones to awaken and open their lives to what the Lord wanted to do in and through them by His Spirit. Even those who were trying were about to give out. There was a real need at Sardis for strong leadership founded upon the clear exposition of God's Word. If they do not wake up and live, devoting themselves to Christian witness and service, if they do not live in expectation of Christ's return, they will not be ready to face Him when He comes without warning.

The city of Philadelphia was considered by the Romans to be their doorway to the East. Therefore, the image of Christ which is applied to the situation of the church there is that of One who holds the key and controls the doorway to God's Kingdom. Indeed, Jesus is Himself the doorway. (John 10:7) In Him, the door to God's Kingdom is open for repentant sinners to enter. The door to justice is open to the downtrodden. The door to truth and to freedom is open to the spiritually or politically oppressed.

It appears that the church at Philadelphia was a group accustomed to oppression, including that from the "synagogue of Satan." Yet, though they have no political clout, though they are rejected by most of the society around them, though they are weak in many ways, they are holding on to the truth of Christ. Perhaps they have little ability, but they are doing the best they can with what they have. That is all the Lord asks of us. He said during His earthly ministry that "he who is faithful in a very little is faithful also in much" (Luke 16:10). So the Lord tells them to keep following their present path of faithfulness and not let anyone take away their crown by turning them away from that path. He promises them that He will preserve them from the coming destruction of the wicked and give them a place of honor and security in His Kingdom, where the character of God, signified by His name, will be seen in them forever.

The "letter" to Laodicea sums up the message that there can be no compromise between devotion to Christ and the demands of the world expressed in the worship of the emperor. As I said earlier, there is no word of praise for this church. The reason is their low level of commitment. They are "neither cold nor hot" but "lukewarm." It appears that their major sin was apathy or indifference and complacency. Other sins have been noted in other churches, and the church in Ephesus has been warned of the possibility that Christ may come and remove them from their place, but none is condemned so forcefully as the complacent Laodiceans, whom Jesus threatens to vomit out of His mouth. Clearly, God can tolerate outright iniquity, even in the Church, much better than He can abide complacency. Say anything to the Lord except "I don't care." You must care if you are to ask for and receive forgiveness.

What was it about the church in Laodicea that evoked this kind of harsh condemnation? Perhaps they had not yet been touched by the severe persecution which others in Asia were experiencing. Why was this? I think they were going unnoticed by their pagan neighbors. They were citizens of a rich banking, textile, and medical manufacturing community. John accuses them of taking the attitude that they are rich and prosperous and in need of nothing. They are a church of very wealthy and self-sufficient people, who apparently are not seeking to reach out into the community to spread the Gospel with any kind of zeal at all. Perhaps they are even using their wealth to buy their way out of persecution, or perhaps they are guilty of attending the required activities of the emperor cult, in order to keep up the appearance of "doing their civic duty" and thus safeguard their positions as prominent citizens in the community. Whatever the case, they are not being persecuted, simply because there is no noticeable difference between them and the pagans around them. There is no zeal and no vital witness for Christ among them. *They* believe, and they think that is good enough. They think they lack nothing, but Jesus says they are "wretched, pitiable, poor, blind, and naked." Their holding of the Faith as mere religion is worthless. They lack the treasure of a lively and challenging witness for Christ. What they hold as faith is therefore a counterfeit, and so they are poor in what is of value to Christ and His Kingdom. Because they enjoy security in this world's scheme of things, they are blind to their own failure to be what Christ expects of His Church.

Jesus counsels them to obtain from Him "gold refined by fire"—the true Faith which no one can be content merely to have and not proclaim. He counsels them to be dressed in "white garments"—the symbol of the triumph and purity of His Gospel. He counsels them to be healed of their spiritual blindness so that their eyes may be opened to the truth. Jesus is calling upon them to wake up to what is going on around them and see that they must finally take a stand. He wants people who are "on fire" for His Gospel. They are guilty of giving intellectual assent to the Gospel, but not letting it make any difference in their lives or their approach to the world. They are not standing up and being counted for Christ. If they are to be acknowledged by Christ, who is "the faithful and true witness," they are going to have to *confront* the evil of this world, not peacefully coexist with it.

Of all the messages in this series of "letters," I think this one is the most urgently applicable to the Church today, at least in America. Of all the problems the Church faces, both outside and within, the most prevalent is the kind of indifference of which the church of Laodicea is accused here. Too many people have taken Jesus Christ into their minds and taken His name onto their lips, but have yet to take Him upon the throne of their hearts. They call themselves Christians and would not worship any other as Lord, but they fail to make the connection between what is said and done in church and what is going on in the world around them. They do not realize that while they may proclaim only Jesus as Lord in their worship services, they allow other people or institutions to take His place as Lord in the daily living of their lives. Most Christians today are not willing to risk the displeasure of government or society by challenging the evils of which government or society may be guilty. Jesus is fine for Sunday morning, but His Lordship is forgotten when it comes to matters such as keeping one's job or maintaining one's citizenship or even popularity. If we can tolerate in silence the evils of this world, if we give in to the peer pressure of those who don't want to be bothered with moral imperatives, if we refuse to take a stand on any issue on the basis of the Word of God as opposed to popular opinion, then it does little good to say that Jesus is Lord of creation, for He has not yet become Lord of our lives. There is no room to be complacent. We are either decidedly for Christ and His standards for living, or we are against Him. There is no middle ground.

While there is no word of praise for the church in Laodicea, and there is harsh condemnation, yet there is a word of hope, although it may be a hard word to hear. "Those whom I love, I reprove and chasten; so be zealous and repent. Behold, I stand at the door and knock; if any one hears my voice and opens the door, I will come in to him and eat with him, and he with me" (Revelation 3:19–20). Human nature finds it hard to believe that a word of condemnation can be, at the same time, an expression of love. But the message that Jesus directs through John to the Pastor at Laodicea, and thus through him to the church, is such a message. He is pointing out what is wrong there, not because He hates them, but because He is fighting to save them from themselves. By their complacency, they are actually resisting Him. Notice that the message is sent first to the Pastor of the church. It is a word which he needs to hear first, and then pass on to the church, for he is responsible to arouse them from their blind indifference. While they remain complacent, the purpose Christ has for them will not be fulfilled. But Jesus does not force His way through the fast-closed door of a complacent heart. He stands at the door and knocks, patiently seeking entrance. We cannot enter the doorway to God's Kingdom until we open the door of our heart and let Jesus come in and throw out all our false lords and gods. He allows us the freedom as the doorkeepers of our hearts to make that decision. If we ever do finally choose to let go of all the things which we have not been willing to risk for the sake of commitment to Him, He will come in and abide with us, and share with us all of our deep desires and fears and dreams and longings. Greater still, He will give us the inner peace of eternal triumph over all things evil—a triumphant faith which simply must be shared, a faith which refuses to compromise with evil, and which will not rest from bearing witness to His truth, so long as one enemy of Christ remains.

In being confronted with this "letter," every church and every Christian is made to face the question of commitment. If we are not making any difference in the world *around* us, what difference have we really allowed Christ to make *within* us? If the enemies of Christ are able to ignore us, how faithful have we really been? Jesus clearly taught His disciples that His enemies in the world would see to it that those who are faithful to Him suffer, just as they made Him suffer. We need to let Christ come in and replace our complacency with zeal. When we do, we find that the treasure of His fellowship is far more precious than anything our commitment to Him might cost us.

I believe that Jesus stands at the door of the Church even today, and knocks with that "nail-scarred hand." We need to let Him in to purge us of our complacency toward so many things, so that we might get busy winning the lost *and* standing up for what is right. So many church people seem so frustrated and aimless in their religious life today. We will remain so until we answer Jesus' knock at the door, let Him in, and begin to do the things we need to do and to be the faithful and true witnesses He calls us to be. It is that image of the glorified Christ from chapter 1 of Revelation that is applied to the church at Laodicea because, by their complacency, they were betraying Him who is "the faithful and true witness, the beginning of God's creation."

Any time we call ourselves Christians, but choose to play it safe and keep silent in the face of evil, we are deserters from the army of the Lord of hosts, traitors against Jesus our King. It was so in Laodicea at the end of the first century, and it is so in every age in every church that is silent when Christ bids them speak or idle when Christ bids them to take action. If only we will hear His call and respond in obedient service, like Dietrich Bonhoeffer in Nazi Germany and Operation Rescue in abortion-defiled America, we shall find that there is no greater reward or personal fulfillment than that of bearing one's own share of Christ's work and even suffering in close and faithful fellowship with Him and with His saints. If only we'll open our hearts to that new life, our lives will find meaning and worth such as nothing else can give. Jesus who is "the beginning of God's creation" is now the beginning of the new creation, in which He calls us to be new creatures. We cannot do that by siding with His old enemies, even by mere silence and inaction.

This reference to Christ as "the beginning of God's creation" is reminiscent of the prologue of John's gospel. This seems to be another piece of evidence that there is a connection between the Fourth Gospel and the Apocalypse. It certainly seems very likely to me that the same man who wrote "In the beginning was the Word, and the Word was with God, and the Word was God" is reminding us of that fact about Jesus in calling Him the beginning of God's creation.

CHAPTER 4

Round the Throne of God (Revelation 4:1–5:14)

In this portion of John's vision, he is blessed with the rare privilege of witnessing the cosmic spectacle of God in His glory as Creator and Christ in His glory as Redeemer being worshipped by the heavens and by the Elders of His people. John sees an open door in heaven and hears the voice of Christ inviting him to enter. This is reminiscent of John's gospel, in which we are told that Jesus Himself said, "I am the door of the sheep." Christ's invitation to John to enter the door to heaven which He has opened symbolizes the fact that Jesus has opened the way to the mercy seat of God for those who are faithful to Him.

John is carried in this vision into the court of the heavenly King, and beholds God upon His eternal throne. It is noteworthy that he does not call God by name, but merely reports that he has seen "a throne…in heaven, with one seated on the throne." In John's Jewish heritage, the name of Yahweh was not pronounced aloud, and there was a great hesitation, even among the prophets, about claiming to have seen God. Mortal, sinful man cannot look upon the face of God and live. To claim to look God in the face would be to claim that one is himself perfect and holy, like God. So it was customary in relating visions of God to avoid describing His own personal appearance, in order not to claim too much for oneself. The impression is that John saw God upon the throne, but did not dare look directly at Him. Of course, it must also be remembered that John is relating a vision, and does not mean to claim that he was actually physically in heaven or actually physically saw God. In fact, it is necessary throughout the Book of Revelation to remind ourselves that this is only a vision, and that things which are presented in symbolic language are not to be understood by taking them literally.

The idea here is that John has been summoned before the King of all creation in order to be shown "what must take place after this." That part of the vision begins in chapter 6. Before John can get around to sharing that knowledge with us, however, he simply must share with us in great excitement and joy this vision of the wonders of creation, giving glory to the Father and to His Christ.

John is awestruck by the glory of God's appearance. He describes that appearance in terms of the brilliance of precious gems. The jasper stone occurs in a variety of colors. John most likely intended to refer to the green jasper, since green is the color symbol of eternal life.[3] The carnelian is a red stone, suggesting fire and perhaps warfare. Yahweh was understood from early on as the God of the storm and the Commander of the hosts of heaven, His army of angels. The Bible also tells us that "our God is a consuming fire" (Hebrews 12:29). We shall see in Revelation that God is at war with His enemies, who will be consumed in His fiery wrath.

In the rainbow that shines round the throne, we have a double symbolism. A rainbow is a symbol of promise, going back to the rainbow which God placed in the sky as a sign of His promise to Noah. This particular rainbow, being green, symbolizes the promise of eternal life. The rainbow is what we see represented in so many religious paintings by a circle of light called a halo. This emerald-green rainbow is not a light shining on the throne of God. It is the light of glory shining from God. When Jesus or some saint is portrayed with a halo around the head, it is the painter's way of saying that that person reflects the glory of God. This rainbow in John's vision glows with the green of eternal life because it shines forth from Him who lives forever and who grants eternal life to those who love Him, according to His promise.

Round the throne of God, John sees twenty-four elders seated upon twenty-four thrones. These are the twelve Patriarchs of Israel and the twelve Apostles of the Church. Thus John's vision stresses the very basic Christian doctrine that the Church is the continuation of the covenant people of God, the New Israel of the New Covenant. The fact that these twenty-four elders are seated on thrones and wear golden crowns means that they reign with God in His Kingdom. The white garments they wear are the symbol of the victory given to them in Christ, by virtue of which they are allowed to reign with Him and to function as His priests. As there were two priests in the Jerusalem Temple for each month, and thus twenty-four for the year, these twenty-four elders are now seen as the celestial leaders of God's people in worshiping Him.[4]

The "flashes of lightning, and voices and peals of thunder," which issue from the throne, symbolize the power and judgment of God. They are reminiscent of the signs of God's presence on Mount Sinai at the time of the giving of the Law. It is recorded in Exodus 19 that, "there were thunders and lightnings, and a thick cloud upon the mountain…and Mount Sinai was wrapped in smoke, because Yahweh descended upon it in fire; and the smoke of it went up like the smoke of a kiln, and the whole mountain quaked greatly… Moses spoke and God answered him in thunder." John intends to leave no doubt that the God to whom the New Israel is united in Jesus Christ is none other than the great God Yahweh, the God of storms, to Whom the Old Israel was bound in the Sinai Covenant.

John sees "seven torches of fire" burning before the throne, which, he says, are "the seven spirits of God." This is another symbolic reference to the Holy Spirit as completely and perfectly God, illuminating the heavenly throne room with the fire of God's glory. Before the throne, there is also a "sea of glass, like crystal." This is the firmament of heaven, which divides heaven from the creation, but through which God sees every thing and every occurrence under heaven.

The "four living creatures, full of eyes in front and behind… all round and within" are constellations. They represent the wonders of the heavens which God has created, which are "for signs and for seasons and for days and for years" (Genesis 1:14). The "eyes" are the stars in the constellations. Each living creature bears a further important meaning. The one with the face of a lion is Leo, which represents strength and power. The one like an ox is Taurus, which represents patient service. The one with a man's face is probably Aquarius, which represents intelligence, and may bear reference to the Holy Spirit, since Aquarius is the water carrier, and the Holy Spirit is symbolized by water. The one like an eagle is Aquila, which represents high spiritual triumph by the symbolism of its high flight. Each of these four characteristics will be sorely needed to sustain the Asian Christians in their coming ordeal. But taken in sum, the four constellations seen as "four living creatures" and thus symbolizing all the living things God has created on earth, as well as the far-flung marvels of the universe, serve to represent the heavens and the earth and all that has life and breath, uniting in praise to the Creator. We are told that they never stop their song of praise. Clearly, John has in mind here the words of the psalmist, "The heavens are telling the glory of God" (Psalm 19:1).

What we have here is a scene of heavenly worship of God. As the "four living creatures give glory and honor and thanks" to God, the twenty-four elders humble themselves before Him in worship. "Glory and honor and thanks" is a threefold ascription of praise. Because God is Three in One, three is the heaven number and stands for truth. The praise which the twenty-four elders render follows the lead of the praise given by the four living creatures, by ascribing to God the threefold blessing of "glory and honor and power." Thus John gives us a picture of the glory and the heavenly worship of God to which the earth and its inhabitants should aspire, as all creation unites in the worship of the one true and living God.

Next, John sees that God is holding in His right hand a scroll which is sealed with seven seals. That is to say that it is completely sealed. It contains information which is completely unknown to any-one but God. This is the scroll of the destiny of the world. He Who made the heavens and the earth holds the fate of all creation in His right hand. It is a mystery to all but Him. God Himself has sealed up this scroll. He has hidden the meaning until there should be one who is worthy and powerful enough to open the seals. But there is said to be no one in heaven or earth, no angel or man, no mere created being, who is able to reveal what God has hidden.

John weeps because the truth of God remains hidden from men. Then one of the elders comforts John by telling him that at last, there is one who is able to open the seals and make known what God has hidden. That one is none other than the Messiah, the victorious "Lion of the tribe of Judah, the Root of David," who is, of course, Jesus Christ. The whole point of this book is for John to make known what Jesus reveals from the scroll in God's right hand, which He alone is deemed worthy to open. That is why the book is called "The Revelation of John."

Recognizing the titles of "Lion of the tribe of Judah" and "Root of David" as references to the promised Davidic king who was expected to establish the Davidic Kingdom of God forever, John looks for a mighty warrior to step forward to open the scroll. Instead of a mighty warrior or fierce lion, John sees an humble Lamb, which, though it has been sacrificed, is yet alive. The Lamb is worthy to open the scroll because He has conquered sin by putting the will of God and the salvation of sinners ahead of His own life, rather than conquering the world by military might that puts its own success ahead of the lives of others. He has conquered death by the power of God Who has rewarded His faithfulness by raising Him from the tomb.

Where John sees this Lamb standing is important. The Lamb stands "between the throne of God and the four living creatures and among the elders." Jesus, the "Lamb of God Who takes away the sins of the world," (John 1:29, 36—another connection here with John's gospel) is the Mediator, the Intercessor between God and His fallen creation. He stands among the twenty-four elders, being the Redeemer of all the elect, both of Old Covenant Israel and of the New Covenant Israel, which together form the eternal Church. It must be remembered that in John's day, they believed that the stars, sun, and moon passed through the sky while the earth stood firm and still. So even though the four living creatures represent constellations and thus the heavens, they are inseparable from the earth in John's understanding. The number 4 is the earth number. The heavenly bodies have no meaning for John apart from their relation to the earth and the cosmic glorification of God. They are part and parcel of the totality of creation together with the earth. The Bible teaches that by man's sin, the whole creation is corrupted and in need of redemption. So the Lamb stands between the judgment throne of God and all of creation. He stands among the elders to stand with them and uphold them, so that by His power and worthiness and authority, they may persevere and reign with Him in His Kingdom.

The Lamb that John sees has seven horns. In apocalyptic and prophetic literature, a horn is a symbol of power, whether it is power used for good or for evil. That the Lamb has seven horns means that His power is complete and perfect. The seven eyes are another representation of the Holy Spirit by Whom, though He is physically absent from us, Jesus is yet present throughout the creation and sees all that is done on earth. With these seven horns and seven eyes, Jesus, the Lamb of God, has perfect and complete power and knowledge to rule over heaven and earth in the name of His Father. It is this highly exalted Lamb, Who was slain and yet lives to redeem the creation, Who, alone, is able to reveal what God has kept hidden until the proper time.

When He steps forward to take the scroll, thus receiving what is rightfully His alone of the glory and mystery of God, the heavens and the earth can contain themselves no longer. They join in breaking forth in praise. The four living creatures and the twenty-four elders prostrate themselves before Him and lead all the angels in heaven and all creation in singing a new song of praise to the Redeemer. In that new song, they praise Him for having ransomed by His self-sacrifice "men for God from every tribe and tongue and people and nation." This again uses the number 4, the earth number, and declares Jesus Lord of the earth Who brings into the Kingdom of God the faithful from all over the earth, regardless of their race or color or national origin.

The vast angelic army of heaven now gives to Jesus the Lamb a song of perfect praise, containing the sevenfold reference to "power and wealth and wisdom and might and honor and glory and blessing." The number 7 represents completeness and perfection by combining the earth number, 4, with the heaven number, 3. Thus the praise of Jesus is perfect because the heavens and the earth become one in worshipping Him.

In John's vision, every inhabitant of all creation eventually acknowledges the Lamb as Redeemer and true Lord of the earth by the fourfold "blessing and honor and glory and might," which they ascribe to Him. When the earth thus acknowledges Him as Lord, the heavens shout "Amen!" and the elders of the elect worship Him still.

From these two chapters of John's vision, we learn that nothing in heaven or on earth goes unnoticed by God, and that nothing is unrelated to Him. Indeed, everyone and everything is subject to His judgment. The destiny of all mankind is subject to God's will and has been placed in the hands of Christ Jesus, the Lamb of God. John's gospel is the only one of the four that tells us of John the Baptizer referring to Jesus in this way. Here, John shows us by using the term again how important it is to his understanding of the Gospel. As the four living creatures and the twenty-four elders and the myriads of angels are gathered round the throne of God in this vision, so all of creation will be gathered round the Lamb when He comes to judge the just and the unjust. John is telling the Asian Christians that God, not Rome, is the center of the universe, that Christ, and not Domitian, is Lord and God. We must worship only the one true and living God, Who reveals Himself to us in the man Jesus, slain as the Lamb for our sin. We are to be gathered in praise round His throne for judgment and grace. The counterfeit glory of Domitian, or of anyone who would turn our allegiance from God, will soon perish, but the Lord Jesus is the Holy One of Israel, Who was and is and is to come, whose glory will never fade.

The day comes when all creation, gathered round the throne of God, will cry aloud something like the sevenfold shout of praise voiced in Revelation 5:12. Then, all troubles and strife forgotten, we shall rejoice round the throne of God eternally, at last giving to God that perfect praise which is the true meaning and goal and purpose of our very lives.

CHAPTER 5

A Vision of the Faithful (Revelation 6:1–8:5)

In Revelation 6:1–8:5, John relates to us that portion of his vision in which the Lamb opens the seven seals of the scroll of destiny. There are three sets of seven judgments each in the Apocalypse. Each set brings a number of plagues upon the wicked, reminiscent of the plagues sent upon Egypt. The seven seals are the first set, the first cycle of God's acts of judgment unleashed upon the earth. The seven seals are divided into a set of four, bearing direct effect upon the earth, and a set of three, giving us a glimpse into the spiritual realm. John tells us about the opening of the first six seals in chapter 6. Before he comes to the opening of the seventh seal, in the first five verses of chapter 8, the seventeen verses of chapter 7 interrupt the sequence of the seven seals to give us a vision of the faithful on earth, and thus to teach us something about what it means to be the Church of Jesus' disciples in a world corrupted by evil.

It is imperative to remember that all this is told in highly symbolic language. These images are not to be taken literally. This is a vision, a dream. As in the dreams of Pharaoh in Genesis, the images we see here are meant to represent something other than what appears on the surface. Just as Joseph did not interpret Pharaoh's dream to mean seven lean cows would literally eat up seven fat cows, but that these images represented seven years of plenty and seven years of famine, we must not interpret John's imagery literally, either. It will never make sense if we do. The Apocalypse must be understood in its symbolic intent, or not at all.

In the opening of the first four seals, a sequence is revealed which is repeated time and again throughout history. The sequence is symbolized by four horsemen. The second, third, and fourth horsemen are to be understood as following the first in natural sequence. The things they represent are to be understood as resulting inevitably from the action of the first horseman.

The white horse represents victory, in this case, the victory of evil. The red horse represents warfare and strife. The black horse represents famine. The horse that is "pale" or greenish gray, the color of a corpse, represents death, and is followed by Hades, which is a universal symbol of the grave.

The rider of the first horse is not Jesus, as some have supposed. It is clear that he is not Jesus, because Jesus does not bring warfare, famine, and death in the wake of His victory. He brings peace, blessings, and life. No, the rider of this white horse is patterned after the Parthians, a warlike people, excellent cavalrymen and archers, who were enemies of Rome, and yet were sometimes employed by Rome to punish a rebellious province. This rider comes forth "conquering and to conquer." He represents no one in particular, but rather all who would seek to enrich themselves by the conquest of others. When such people are victorious, their victory always means the destruction of peace, which results in famine, which further extends death beyond the battlefield. The evil of those who seek to conquer for their own enrichment and empowerment always brings desolation and death to the innocent. Seeking to build themselves up by force, they destroy far more than they build. Surely, such individuals or nations cannot be thought of as God's servants. However, they are often the instrument by which He accomplishes His judgment on the wicked, as when the Assyrians were used to punish Israel and the Babylonians were used to punish Judah. But the point is that whenever we seek to conquer by our own power, to further our own unrighteous ambitions, only destruction and disaster can come of it. Christ alone leaves good in the wake of His victory, for He sets out to conquer the things that take life away from us. He fights for our good, unlike earthly conquerors who will destroy anyone who gets in the way of their selfish ambitions.

The truth of this symbolism is easily attested by history. We need only think of the Assyrians, the Babylonians, the Persians, the Romans, the Parthians, the Huns, the Vikings, the Japanese Empire and the Nazis in World War II, the Soviets, and yes, even the butchering of American Indians by the white man in America's westward expansion. It also holds true on a small scale, at least in a spiritual sense, whenever certain individuals or groups seek to dominate those around them, and thereby bring conflict and desolation to their own family, neighborhood, or church. Even though God may use the unjust conqueror to accomplish His own purpose of judgment, His mercy is indicated by the injunction given to the third horseman not to harm oil and wine, and by only a fourth of the earth being given over to the power of Death and Hades. That is to say that even though God in His judgment of sinful humanity may allow our own wicked strife to cause widespread destruction, in His mercy, He limits the power of those destructive forces so that some may be spared. The oil and wine represent blessings from God to bolster His people even during disasters.

In the opening of the fifth seal, the scene changes from earth to heaven. Here, we see that the blood of those who die in the persecution because they are faithful unto death cries out to God for justice, even as the blood of Abel cried out to God from the ground when Cain slew him. This is a symbolic way of assuring John's readers that even if they die in the persecution, they are secure in God's hand if they are loyal to Christ. The victory will yet be theirs as symbolized by the white robes they are given. This is meant to encourage the readers to remain faithful, even in the face of death. It is a way of saying that, even though they die at the hands of infidels on earth, their martyrdom is accounted as a holy sacrifice upon God's own altar in heaven. The judgment that God will bring upon their persecutors will be vindication of His faithful witnesses, who inherit His victory of eternal life.

The word usually translated "souls" in this passage, as elsewhere, actually means "lives." The Bible knows nothing of an "immortal soul." The Old Testament teaches us that "the blood is the life." John does not mean to say that some immortal essence has gone to heaven and cries out to God from the altar in the heavenly temple. He is referring symbolically to the blood of the martyrs as their lives being poured out on the altar of devotion to Jesus. He is saying that the atrocity of shedding their blood cries out to God for justice.

Following immediately upon this assurance that the vindication for which the blood of the martyrs cries out will certainly come, the sixth seal is opened, and the power of God's judgment is revealed. So great is God's wrath against His enemies who seek to destroy His people that it threatens to shatter the universe. So terrible is His judgment that the wicked who have persecuted His people and rejected His Son seek to be smashed under the rocks of a crumbling world, rather than have to face the fierce anger of the Lamb. Here is a clear warning that because God's grace in Jesus Christ is so perfectly offered to everyone, the holiness of God necessitates that His judgment upon those who reject His grace must be as great as His mercy to those who accept it. Because they reject His Christ and persecute His Church, the wrath of God is about to be unleashed upon the wicked.

Here, the sequence is interrupted. The actual enactment of God's final judgment upon the wicked is not yet. What has been presented so far is only symbolic representation of His judgment. In 8:5, the application of God's wrath begins to be seen. The next sequence of plagues, the seven trumpets, will be introduced in 8:1–5 and set in motion when the curse of the seventh seal is completed. That curse of the seventh seal is the actual coming of God's judgment to earth out of heaven as an angel throws down upon the earth a golden censer containing incense mingled with the prayers of the saints and fire from God's heavenly altar. This results in "peals of thunder, loud noises, flashes of lightning, and an earthquake." These are all symbols of Yahweh's presence, power, and judgment, as revealed on Mount Sinai at the time the Ten Commandments were given. This display strikes terror in the hearts of God's enemies as He comes to destroy them and vindicate His saints. But before the seventh seal is opened and the wrath of God is finally unleashed upon the earth, the command comes to delay the judgment until the seal of God has been placed upon all of His servants to exempt them from the destruction that befalls the wicked and the creation which they have corrupted.

In chapter 7, as the sequence of the seven seals is interrupted and the coming of God's judgment delayed, John shares with us a vision of the faithful who are to be spared the destruction which God's wrath is about to bring upon the earth and all who deny Him. Here is one of the places in this book where certain people and groups, such as the Jehovah's Witnesses, bring in false teachings based on an unwarranted literalism in interpreting what is a very nonliteral, highly allegorical piece of Christian literature. I'm sure you have heard the claim that there will only be 144,000 people saved. That is based upon a very irresponsible and incomplete reading of the text. If you read closely enough, it is very simple to see that John talks about at least two distinct groups of the faithful who are to be sealed. The 144,000 refers only to the faithful among the Jews. It is not a literal figure even then. It is an allegorical way of saying that before the final judgment comes, all of the Jews who are going to accept Jesus as Lord will do so. The number is only symbolic, representing the whole number of the redeemed of Israel, without indicating an exact number as many wrongly suppose it does.

John arrived at this number by multiplying the square of the Church number, 12, which equals 144, by the cube of the round number, 10, which is 1,000. Even if it were to be taken as a literal number, it only refers to Christian Jews, and thus does not represent the total number of all the redeemed. Those who say that it does are overlooking verse 9, in which John tells us of "a great multitude which no man could number, from every nation, from all tribes and peoples and tongues." These are the faithful among the Gentiles, a mass of people from all over the world, in numbers beyond human calculation. These, together with the 144,000 sealed among the Jews, are by faith the true descendants of Abraham, to whom God promised descendants as innumerable as the stars in the sky or the grains of sand by the sea. It is obvious that John expected something far beyond a literal 144,000 to be redeemed.

It is interesting to note that in the list of the tribes of Israel in this chapter, Judah is named first, ahead of Ruben, Jacob's firstborn. This sequence appears only here among all of the Bible's listings of the twelve tribes. John wants it to be clear that the Lamb in his vision is none other than the Christ, descended from David, of the tribe of Judah, and that it is thus through Judah that the plan of salvation is advanced.

The thing that is important about the 144,000 among the Jews and the innumerable throng among the Gentiles is not their exact number, but the fact that they are faithful. They are the ones who patiently endure the persecution of a corrupt world, and through it all, even if it means death, cling steadfastly to Christ Jesus as their Lord. In John's vision, those who are faithful are "sealed" with the seal of God in order to be spared the coming destruction, just as in Egypt, those who smeared the blood of a lamb on their doorposts were spared when the angel of death passed over them.

It is important to understand that this sealing of the faithful is to spare them from the wrath of God. It assures them that whatever they endure, even death, they are secure in God's hand. His destruction of the earth and of all who reject Him will not touch them because they have received the grace of the Lamb in faith, having "washed their robes and made them white in the blood of the Lamb." They are dressed in white because the Lamb's victory of perfect obedience and eternal life has become their victory. However, the sealing of the faithful is only to exempt them from God's wrath. It does not exempt them from the wrath of men. Here is a sobering lesson for us to learn in a day when most church members wouldn't dare to take a stand they thought would offend anyone. The lesson is that our security in Christ, our hope of eternal glory, often lies in our passing with Him through great tribulation. John foresaw evil days coming upon those who would stand for Christ and refuse to allow another to sit upon the Lord's throne. He, therefore, tells His readers in the churches of Asia that they must remain faithful to Jesus and openly claim Him as Lord, without fear of the persecution they will endure.

For, if they are faithful, they will be spared the far worse tribulation of the wrath of God and share the victory of His Kingdom. There, no more harm can come to them as they constantly serve and praise Him forever.

Now, this does not mean you have to die for your faith in order to be redeemed. It does mean, however, that you must be that loyal and faithful. It means that even if you never have to face a Domitian or a Hitler, as did the first century martyrs or Dietrich Bonhoeffer in Nazi Germany, even if you do not die at the hands of the wicked because you refuse to acknowledge another man in Christ's place, the way you *live* must be as faithful to Christ as the way Bonhoeffer and Peter and Paul and countless other martyrs have *died*.

John's Apocalypse shows us that to be faithful means to endure tribulations for the sake of Christ and the victory that is ours in Him. Thus, it is like other apocalyptic literature in its call for faithfulness. However, whereas other apocalyptic writings called for armed resistance to the enemy, John's Apocalypse is instead a call to patient endurance. It is a call to continue to proclaim and to live the Gospel faithfully and peacefully, come what may. What makes the call for this kind of patient endurance of tribulation valid, as opposed to a call to armed resistance, is the assurance that we need not fight an enemy whom Christ has already defeated. That is, we need not fight the true Enemy, Satan, with acts of violence against his servants. We can be patiently faithful because even though we may die, in Christ, the victory of eternal life is already ours. Thus, we are to fight the enemy through deeds of love and mercy and compassion. For these are the weapons of Christ upon the cross against the evil of human sin and selfishness, and against Satan.

CHAPTER 6

The Undoing of the Creation (Revelation 8:6–9:21)

As he did in the case of the seven seals, John divides the judgments of the seven trumpets into a set of four and a set of three, with a delay between the sixth and seventh trumpets. In each case, he shows the relationship between earthly and heavenly events—that natural and supernatural truths cannot be so neatly separated as to be without mutual significance and effect. However, the events that are summoned by the first four trumpets emphasize a different aspect of God's judgment upon the earth than what was emphasized by the horsemen of the first four seals. The four horsemen were meant to represent the fact that God sometimes brings judgment upon the earth by simply allowing the greedy and malevolent pursuits of sinful men to bear their natural fruits of warfare or strife, famine and death. In the symbolism of the four trumpets, however, we see that God does not always merely leave men to their own evil devices. In addition to allowing the evil deeds of mankind to enact His judgment upon us through the inevitable working out of the consequences of our iniquity, God at times performs mighty acts of terrible punishment, according to John's vision.

John does not intend to say that God exhausts one method of judgment before implementing the other. The sequence in which he has given the two different accounts of these two different aspects of

God's execution of judgment upon us is unimportant in that respect. Both kinds of judgment are going on all the time. The only significance to the order in which John presents the two forms of judgment is that the seven trumpets arise out of the seven seals, which means that even God's own specific and terrifying acts of judgment are necessitated and made unavoidable by man's sin, just as is true of the inevitable consequences of our actions, in which God does not act quite so directly. In other words, there is judgment built into the creation, to the effect that as we ignore the rules God has laid out for our living as part of His creation, we bring trouble on ourselves, as Paul points out in Romans 1:26–27.

Yet, sooner or later, God Himself is moved to respond directly to our iniquity at various times with specific acts of His own, which will culminate in the great conflagration in the final judgment, as predicted by Peter in II Peter 3:10–12.

In the series of the first four trumpets, God sends upon the unrighteous world plagues that are very similar to some of the ones visited upon Egypt through Moses. Specifically, there is a plague of "hail and fire, mixed with blood," which would correspond to the plague of hail which turned into fire as it hit the ground when Moses called for it at God's command. Then there are the two plagues which affect the water of the seas and rivers and springs, just as through Moses, God had smitten the waters of Egypt. The fourth trumpet brings a plague of darkness, such as God had sent upon Egypt. Here, the important thing is not any effect upon the sun, moon and stars themselves, but the fact that their light is withdrawn from the earth.

There is a great deal of significance in the similarity between these plagues to be brought upon the Roman Empire and those which had fallen upon Egypt. It means that the Author of these acts of judgment is indeed the same God who had redeemed the children of Israel from slavery. Just as He had made war upon Egypt to set His people free, John is saying that God will also make war upon the Roman Empire to vindicate and save His new people, the Christians who refuse to serve any other god. It also means that just as the Hebrews did not raise a hand in their own defense against the Egyptians, even so the Christians who are oppressed by Rome are to endure their troubles peacefully and trust in the Lord to do battle for them. One other connection that should not be overlooked is the fact that all of the plagues brought upon Egypt addressed gods of the Egyptians, and in each case showed Yahweh to be superior to any other possible god. Surely, part of the message in these four trumpets is the application of this fact to the ridiculous claim of Domitian that he is Zeus incarnate. Of course, the difference is that John, unlike the enslaved Hebrews, knows that there is no other god but the one living and true God, who has made Himself known in Jesus Christ.

When the fifth trumpet is blown, the "shaft of the bottom-less pit" is opened, so that the evil it holds may be unleashed upon the earth to punish the wicked. Now, this bottomless pit is a very important image in Jewish thought of the time. It relates back to the great flood in the days of Noah. It was generally believed in John's day that there was more involved in the flood than the rain that fell from the sky. They believed that the waters which were normally confined beneath the earth were allowed to rise from "the bottomless pit," as well. What is important about this idea, and what affords such an apt application of the imagery here in John's vision is that this rising of the subterranean waters represented the reversal of the orderliness God had imposed upon His creation in the beginning.

We usually talk about God creating all things out of nothing. I believe that is indeed the correct understanding of what happened. Contrary to the opinions of some modern scientists, matter is not eternal. There was a time before time when nothing existed but God, and God created all material and spiritual realities other than Himself, without any resources available to Him, where nothing existed before. However, there is more to the story of Genesis 1:1–2:4a than this. The acts which the writer describes there amount to more than the creation of the component parts of the universe. Genesis 1:2 says, "The earth was without form and void, and darkness was upon the face of the deep." What this means is that until God took further action beyond the mere creation of the raw materials of the earth and the heavens, the creation was in a state of chaos. From the time the writer tells us that God said, "Let there be light," the rest of that passage is as much as anything else that particular writer's way of glorifying God by proclaiming that He won the victory over chaos and established order in the creation. That he tells us that God said of the lights in the sky, "let them be for signs and for seasons and for days and for years," is a testimony to the writer's faith in the good and holy God who was wise enough and powerful enough to give order to His creation. The reason that this is such an important idea is that our very lives are so completely dependent upon that orderliness. The forces of chaos threaten our very survival. How good it is to know that the God we worship, the only true God, has overcome the chaos! The people to whom John was writing were facing the overturning of the order they had known by the Roman emperor who disregarded the customary Roman tolerance for religious freedom. In the midst of this chaos, they needed the assurance John was giving them that, as Paul had said, nothing in earth or heaven can overpower God's love and grace toward us who are redeemed. (Romans 8:37–39)

The common understanding of the Jews in John's day concerning the rising of the subterranean waters in the great flood was that in allowing these waters thus to overreach their appointed bounds, God had relaxed the orderliness of His creation just enough to allow the chaos of uncontrolled nature to destroy the wicked. That is precisely why the image of the bottomless pit is so important to John's message here, because in his vision, he sees God doing the same thing again. In this part of the vision, God is unleashing His own and mankind's old enemy, the forces of chaos, to destroy those who reject his sovereign Lordship and persecute His Church.

God made a covenant promise to mankind through Noah that He would never again destroy the earth by water. So, this time, instead of water, it is the host of other forces of chaos which He lets loose to destroy His enemies. For out of the smoke that pours forth from the bottomless pit arises an enormous swarm of locusts, which torture God's enemies. The designated time of their reign of terror is five months, which is merely a symbolic way of saying that the torture will continue only for a very limited time. It is to be noted that only those who have not been sealed with the seal of God are to be affected by these horrors, just as in the Passover, only those who failed to smear their doorposts with lamb's blood lost their firstborn.

Of course, the mention of locusts again causes us to relate these acts of judgment to the plagues sent upon Egypt, which included an invasion of locusts such as the world has never seen before or since. But these particular locusts are a very definite symbol of chaos, also. In God's orderly creation, as a general rule, one species is kept genetically separate from others. But these locusts are clear symbols of chaos in that they are such an unholy mixture. They are like horses but have human faces, women's hair, lions' teeth, scales, and tails with stingers, like scorpions. Their king is apparently a fallen angel, named Abaddon in Hebrew and Apollyon in Greek, which means "the Destroyer."

When the sixth trumpet is blown, more of the forces of chaos are released, this time from beyond "the great river, Euphrates." It is clear that these "twice ten thousand times ten thousand" troops also represent chaos because of the horses they ride, which are, again, an unholy mixture. The horses have lion heads, pouring forth fire and smoke and sulfur, and tails like serpents, with heads that bite. There is yet another important image conveyed by these troops. Because they come from beyond the Euphrates, which was the recognized limit of the Roman Empire, where the Parthian domain began, these troops are clearly meant to be understood as Parthian or similar barbarian invaders, an ever-present potential threat to the order and peace of the Roman Empire. Thus, with the releases of the four angels and the resulting release of this "Parthianesque" horde, the greatest fears of the Romans are realized, at least in John's vision. This is a very apt image for John's message. For if the Parthians had ever dared to cross the Euphrates and make war on Rome, they would surely have thrown the empire into a state of chaos and panic as no other single force on earth could have done.

To sum up all of this, the vision which John presents to us is one of such great acts of judgment upon the Roman Empire that it would seem even to threaten to undo the creation, so great would be the forces of chaos unleashed to punish the wicked oppressors of God's faithful ones. He gives us a picture here of God, in His righteous judgment upon His enemies who afflict His Church, using the forces of chaos which He had Himself subdued in the act of creation, to bring about the beginning of the end of the creation. When mankind rejects God's Lordship, God gives us no choice but that it also means the rejection of His orderly design of the creation. Thus, man's sin breeds chaos. So, if freedom from God's laws is what we want, that is what He will give us. The problem is that that means chaos. John tells us that to deal with such wickedness, God will unleash chaos to destroy the wicked. We want freedom without God. But there can be no freedom without life, and there can be no life without the God who creates life and establishes the order of creation to support it. So, our only chance for true freedom is in following the design and regulations God has given us for life in His world.

John is pointing us toward an eventual time when, for the sake of mankind's wickedness, God will, indeed, unleash such chaos that it will even undo the creation. Yet, we who have faith in Jesus are not to fear. We have the mark of God's ownership and favor upon us. If He Who has such authority and power as to judge the world and to use even His enemies to accomplish His own will is as completely devoted to our redemption as He has shown Himself to be in Jesus upon the cross, what can there be for us to fear? The undoing of the creation is to make room for the new creation, which Christ will bring into perfection when He comes again.

In the meantime, God is continually allowing and causing various forms of evidence of His judgment to threaten to punish the wicked. He is doing so, instead of bringing the world to an end immediately, in order to give all the peoples fair warning and opportunity to repent and be spared in the final judgment. But as John points out, most often, the truly wicked, who have lowered themselves to subhuman levels of evil, turn deaf ears and blind eyes to God's warnings. They will not be spared. In case you are wondering about the accuracy of John's prophecy of judgment on Rome, let me point out that while it was not the Parthians who destroyed Rome and the Empire, it was done by bands of very similar barbarian invaders.

The judgments of God are fearsome, but those who live in Jesus need not fear the terrors that await the wicked. Rather, we have a job to do. Not all who are presently living as enemies of God are beyond being reached. We have the task of warning and rescuing those whom we can convince of the truth of the Gospel. We are meant to be God's people, salvaging what we can of the people of this dying world to share the joy of eternal life. The wickedness of mankind, as opposed to the holiness of God, makes it unavoidable that the final judgment, the undoing of the creation, must come. But because God is a God of love and mercy, He is delaying that final day and sending us into the world with the Gospel to call other sinners like ourselves to repentance and salvation from the destruction that is to come. God calls us to perform this task by living lives of peace, love and assistance to others, such as will draw them to the Gospel, as well as by the proclamation of Jesus Christ as Lord.

We are to make disciples for Jesus by the way we live, knowing that we are saving them from eternal destruction. John was predicting that Rome would soon suffer a small sample of what God's wrath could be like. He wanted the Christians to be aware that if they were going to convert any of the enemies of the Lord to be His disciples, they could not compromise the Faith by calling Domitian Lord or by acts of violence. They must display the Christian life for which they were suffering, not give themselves over to worldly vengefulness, if they hoped to lead anyone to the Lord through their ordeal. John is showing us here the urgency of our witness. Elsewhere, Peter wrote, "Since all these things are thus to be dissolved, what sort of persons ought you to be in lives of holiness and goodness?" (II Peter 3:11). We ought to be the sort of persons in whom the love of God in Jesus Christ is made real to others, even to those who make themselves our enemies. It is our mission as God's chosen people to lead the lost, as we have been led, to the light of God's love and the throne of His grace. This is a dying world. We are sent into the midst of it to lead others to the Christ Who gives new life. We must do this by sharing His love, even in the face of evil, and we must do it now! Tomorrow may be too late. John's vision urges us to realize that even as God is moving toward the undoing of the creation in the final judgment, He calls us to be a part of His work in joining others to the new creation which He has already begun.

CHAPTER 7

Whose Kingdom Is This?
(Revelation 10:1–11:19)

As was the case in the cycle of the seven seals, John here interrupts the cycle of the seven trumpets between number 6 and number 7 to share other images from his vision. The purpose for this aspect of John's apocalyptic style is twofold. First, it gives a dramatic effect in making us wait to see how the cycle will end. Second, it teaches us that God's schedule is not necessarily the same as ours or what we might expect. What may seem a delay to us is not so to Him because for God, all times are present. The uncertainties that keep us in suspense, wondering what God is going to do in the world, and when He will act, and how He will deal with the wicked, are not uncertainties to Him. We have to learn to trust God because He knows what He's doing, even if we don't.

In this interlude between the sixth and seventh trumpets, John first sees "another mighty angel coming down from heaven, wrapped in a cloud, with a rainbow over his head." The cloud is again a symbol of God's judgment, and the rainbow a symbol of God's promise of grace and also a reflection of God's glory. Though it may seem strange to some, it is quite fitting that the messenger who bears the word of God's judgment also bears the word of God's grace. Some people don't want to accept that. They want to hear all about God's mercy, but deny that there is such a thing as damnation. Yet, if judgment were not necessary, there would be no need for grace, either. There would be no Gospel for us to proclaim if the wrath of God were not indeed coming against the wickedness of mankind. Jesus would not have needed to die on the cross to save us from sin if we were not in danger of eternal judgment and the fire of hell. So, with God and His messengers, there is no separating the word of grace from the word of judgment. The grace of Jesus upon the cross is not a game or a mere symbolic act because the sin so many, even in many pulpits of the Church, wish to deny, is a reality. Both judgment and grace, both condemnation and justification, have to do with the reality of sin.

This heavenly messenger whom John sees stands on land and sea, symbolizing God's power over all the realms of earth, and especially the authority over all governments, symbolized by the sea, and all religion, symbolized by the land. He offers assurance of the coming fulfillment of the words of the prophets, all in God's good time, and thus without any real delay, though it appears to us that it is slow in coming.

It is interesting, if a bit frustrating, that John is told to "Seal up what the seven thunders have said, and do not write it down." Could this have been some specific message concerning John himself, which was too personal for him to include here? Could it have been yet another cycle of seven terrors, too terrible to be written down? It sparks curiosity. I'd love to know just what was said to John that God did not want John to record. Perhaps it is best that we don't know. It is sufficient to say that God Himself spoke to John of some mystery that was for John's ears only. The "seven thunders," of course, is a symbolic reference to the voice of Yahweh. It is the perfect utterance of the God Whose power is displayed in the storm.

The heavenly messenger whom John sees standing on sea and land holds an open scroll. Unlike the scroll of destiny, which only the Lamb could unroll, this is a scroll of prophecy already open for John to receive its truth which he must declare. John is commanded to eat the scroll, as also happened to Ezekiel in one of his visions. (Ezekiel 3:1–3) This means that he had to "digest" it—to make the truth that was revealed to him part of himself. This is such a good picture of a prophet or true spokesman for God in any age. There are no more prophets, but those who preach the Word of God faithfully today may be said to have a prophetic ministry, as if inherited from the prophets, so long as their preaching is true to what God revealed to the prophets in times past. When a man or woman is faithful to that calling, the Word of God becomes a part of him or her, and he or she loves more than anything to proclaim the glory and holiness of the righteous God. However, the truth of God, which is "sweet as honey" in one's mouth, must be proclaimed in the world of sinful men. John must "prophesy about many peoples and nations and tongues and kings." Thus, what is sweet in the preacher's mouth makes his stomach bitter because the righteousness of God simply cannot be proclaimed to a sinful world without becoming a judgment on mankind, and the prophet or preacher becomes sickened by the judgment he must repeatedly declare. Yet, however bitter his task of proclamation may become, he simply must continue to receive and absorb and declare God's truth. It is a compulsion that can only be even partially understood by those who are overtaken by it. God is in control, and His truth will prevail, whether the preacher finds it pleasant or not. Jeremiah grew weary of continually having to proclaim God's judgment and bear the hatred of those who refused to listen. He wanted to stop, but he said, "If I say, 'I will not mention Him, or speak any more in His name,' there is in my heart as it were a burning fire shut up in my bones, and I am weary with holding it in, and I cannot" (Jeremiah 20:9). This was John's experience, and it has been mine, as well.

The measuring of the temple is a symbol that the true worship of God places His people in a relationship with Him sufficient to sustain them in the midst of their troubles. The outer court, which was always designated as a place of worship for the Gentiles, is not measured in this instance because the Gentiles, the nations—specifically the Romans—have desecrated it, so that it no longer qualifies as such a place of worship. At the time of John's writing, the Jerusalem Temple had been destroyed about twenty-five years earlier by the Romans, who were still dominating most of the known world. Because the Romans thus oppressed Israel and the emperor,

Domitian, was beginning his persecution of Christians, John considered their rule to be a time of great evil and an affront to God. But he assured his readers that there would be an end to it. The Romans' oppression of God's people would last only "forty-two months." This was not to be taken as a literal figure. John was not predicting a specific actual time when the Roman Empire would fall. "Forty-two months" is three-and-a-half years. Since three and a half is only half of seven, the number of completeness, forty-two months, being three-and-a-half years, symbolizes a limited time. It is a way of saying that the rule of Rome is not of an enduring quality. It is to say that these evil days will not last forever because God, the true Ruler of all nations, will put an end to Roman rule.

Even during the time that the evil of Rome is allowed to flourish as a judgment upon sinful humanity, God is not silent. John tells us of two witnesses who are to "prophesy for 1,260 days." That is, of course, the same symbolic figure as the forty-two months. The idea is that even through the times of evil, God does not leave Himself without a witness. There is never any excuse for those who continue to set themselves against God because there is always someone proclaiming His truth before the world, even in the worst of times. It is significant that there are two witnesses because in a court of law, one witness is not enough. There must be at least two, as God commanded Moses and Israel. Here, it is seen that God abides by His own law.

These two witnesses are clearly patterned after Moses and Elijah, the two greatest prophets of ancient Israel. It was they who appeared with Jesus in the Transfiguration, symbolizing the fulfillment of the Law and the Prophets in Jesus the Christ, and thus serving as witnesses to attest His divine identity. Whoever the two witnesses are whom John had in mind, he is claiming that they and their testimony are as reliable as Moses and Elijah, whom God confirmed before the people by giving them the power to perform wonders, such as shutting up the sky or calling down fire or plagues from heaven. Possibly, the two witnesses he has in mind are Stephen and James, whom we know were executed as martyrs at Jerusalem, the city to which John refers as "Sodom and Egypt, where their Lord was crucified." What John tells us about these two witnesses confirms that, as Jesus triumphed over death and the evil of this world, so shall those who are faithful to Him unto death. The enemies of God rejoiced over the death of Jesus. They rejoice over the deaths of His saints. But by raising Jesus from the grave and, in this vision, raising His slain witnesses, God vindicates them. This strikes terror in the hearts of the wicked because it means that the judgment of God at which they had scoffed is real, after all, and they are doomed. That the two witnesses are taken up to heaven in a cloud, and that this is accompanied by disasters falling upon the wicked, is John's allegorical way of saying that the faithful will be given the same vindication our Lord received, and that the faithfulness of the martyrs is, in itself, a pronouncement of judgment upon the wicked. Some who study this passage run on with all sorts of speculation as to who these two witnesses will be, expecting a literal fulfillment of this passage in the future by two modern-day witnesses who will be executed and return to life in the sight of their murderers. This approach, however, ignores the basic fact that the Apocalypse is allegorical, and does not need a literal fulfillment to be rightly understood and convey its intended message. Again, taking Revelation literally misses the whole point of it.

Finally, John comes to the seventh trumpet, which evokes more heavenly worship of God, in which it is declared that "the kingdom of this world has become the Kingdom of our Lord and of His Christ." God is praised for asserting His authority to overthrow His enemies and establish His own rule upon earth. Thus, as the heavenly temple is opened, there is the ark of the covenant, to show that God still preserves His covenant and His covenant people.

What all these judgments and praise of God reveal is that, regardless of the appearance of things, He is still Lord, in control of creation and history. This is important for John's original readers and for us. They are living in what seems to them a world gone mad. (Sounds familiar, doesn't it?) Their own countrymen have mistreated them for many years because they would not worship the Roman emperor. Now, the emperor Domitian himself is mounting his own campaign of persecution against Christians. They have heard the stories of how Yahweh had often rescued the people of Israel from their enemies. But now they were finding no relief for their suffering at the hands of the wicked. They might very understandably be starting to ask themselves, "Whose kingdom is this world? Does it belong to God or Domitian?"

John is urging them not to lose heart or falter in their faith because of the evil times that are upon them. He seeks to assure them that, just as Christ lay in the darkness of the tomb for only a short few days, even so, there will be a limit to the time that the wicked will triumph over them. There will be an end to their darkness. Although the Romans may seem to rule the world with impunity, John assures his readers that God is indeed the true Ruler. Though it may seem long to them, the rule of Rome will soon end, as the God and Father of our Lord Jesus Christ reclaims His Kingdom and rains judgment upon those who oppress His people.

No matter how strong our faith may be, there are times in our lives when we, too, may begin to wonder, "Whose kingdom is this?" We have so little control over so much of our lives.

There is so much pain and suffering to be endured. We lose loved ones or become ill ourselves. We see or hear of so much evil around us. We can't even seem to control our own thoughts and actions much of the time. It is often as if some external evil force has a stronghold on our lives. We are discouraged and tempted to despair in the face of so much evil and misfortune. It seems our troubles will never end.

John's words convey the very Word of God to us that regardless of what ills we must endure, regardless of how formidable are the forces that threaten us, even death is not to be so feared as to destroy our faithfulness to God in Christ. Death and sin and all other evils are conquered enemies for us because through Jesus Christ, our God has determined their end. This is His Kingdom. Because we know that our Lord has conquered even the grave, we know that even our worst fears and sufferings are as mere passing shadows before the eternal God Who is our King. He is our Father. He is our Redeemer. We are meant to share in His glory. We are intended for life and victory in Christ. Beyond the darkness of the present evils of this world, beyond the terrors of the grave, those who endure in faithfulness to the end will live forever in the peace and joy of a new world that will never end.

But a decision must be made by each of us. This world is God's Kingdom as a matter of objective fact. But we must each decide whether we truly believe it. If we would know the peace and freedom of facing all the good and evil of this life unafraid, in the confidence of faith in God's grace, we must each decide what will be the answer to the question in terms of our own lives, as well as in terms of the universe: "Whose Kingdom is this?" We must decide, as we remember that Jesus said, "The Kingdom of God is in your midst." You must ask yourself, "Is my life God's Kingdom?" If it is, the Word of God assures us that our suffering will soon be over when our Lord is made known at His second coming. So hang on! Believe! By faith, His Kingdom is ours!

Chapter 8

The Adversary
(Revelation 12:1–17)

Up to this point in John's Apocalypse, there has been a great deal of pronouncement of judgment upon the enemies of God and proclamation of the ultimate triumph of Christ. But there has been little or no information as to just what has prompted John to write these things, and just what it is that he is calling upon his readers patiently to endure. In my first seven chapters, I have given you an advantage over John's original readers because I have already told you that John is condemning and proclaiming God's judgment upon the Roman Empire. The Asian Christians who first received this book from John almost certainly had no idea what he was talking about up to this point, and probably only a very limited idea of what he was talking about by the time they finished reading the book. They had the same disadvantage that we have today in trying to understand this bizarre composition. They were gentiles, as are most modern Christians, with no background for understanding Jewish apocalyptic literature. Probably few, if any of them, had read Daniel or Ezekiel or other such highly allegorical Jewish writings. Most of them, therefore, probably did not know what to make of the very strange imagery John employed, any more than do most people today.

However well or poorly his readers were able to understand John's message, here in chapter 12, he finally begins to explain the problem that he is addressing. Any educated Jewish Christian in John's day would likely have had no trouble seeing just what John was talking about in what seems almost like fanciful nonsense to us. But John was writing to Gentile Christians. As we modern Christians study this writing, it will be helpful for us to bear in mind what we can only hope someone explained to its original recipients: that through these very symbolic and nonliteral images, John was giving them a Christian perspective on what he understood as very literal realities.

The first image in chapter 12 is that of a very strange and lovely woman, "clothed with the sun, with the moon under her feet, and on her head a crown of twelve stars." This woman is the Church. That is made clear by the number of stars in her crown, the number 12, which is the numerological symbol for the Church. That she is clothed with the sun and has the moon under her feet indicates that the Church is endowed with great spiritual power and filled with the light of God's glory from on high, as earth and heaven are united in Christ.

This woman, representing the Church, is depicted as being in great travail to give birth. We shall give more attention to that presently. First, we note that standing before her, waiting to devour the child she is about to deliver, is "a great red dragon, with seven heads and ten horns, and seven diadems upon his heads." I shall begin to explain the significance of all these heads and horns and diadems in the next chapter. There are other pressing matters to be explained in this chapter. For now, it is enough to point out what I am sure you already know, that this great red dragon is a symbol for Satan. The sweeping down of a third of the stars of heaven with his tail is a depiction of his efforts and intentions to destroy all the works of God, taking a third of the angels of heaven with him in his rebellion against God, and of his power which is so great that he seems almost capable of doing so. It is the great enemy of God, then, who stands before the woman, waiting to devour her child as it is delivered. Through this symbolism, John declares that Satan, the enemy of God, is the enemy of God's Church, and that he is at work in the world, behind the scenes, in all the troubles that are coming upon the Church.

The name "Satan" is the personification of the Hebrew word which means "adversary." The Bible pictures Satan throughout as the opponent of God and the accuser of man as in a court of law. We see him in the book of Job, wandering through the earth, seeking evidence of man's rebellion against God so that he might come to God and rub man's sin in God's face. When he comes across Job, and finds him to be nearly perfect in his righteousness toward God, he makes up his mind that he simply must destroy Job. He simply can't abide anyone who has such a good relationship with God. He just has to find a way to mess it up. He sets about trying to destroy Job's faith in God so that he will commit the unpardonable sin of cursing God and die as a result. He comes to God and accuses Job of insincerity, saying that Job loves God only for the sake of all the blessings he has received from Him, and not really for God Himself. Thus, Satan is pictured as some kind of self-appointed district attorney of heaven, continually accusing men, "day and night before our God," in the heavenly court, while he himself does all he can to encourage mankind to sin all the more. His whole intention is to overthrow the rule of God in heaven and earth by any means he can employ, particularly by destroying the relationship between God and man.

When the woman who symbolizes the Church gives birth, we are told that her child is a "male child, one who is to rule all the nations with a rod of iron." The dragon seeks to devour this child, but the child is "caught up to God and to His throne." This child is Jesus the Christ. In His infancy, Satan sought to destroy Him through the slaughter of all the male children, two years old and younger, by the hand of Herod. After His baptism, Satan came to Him in the wilderness and sought to destroy Him by tempting Him to renounce His Father God by taking care for His own comfort and prestige and bowing down to Satan. When He was crucified, Satan sought to destroy Him through the jeers of the mob who taunted Him and challenged Him to save Himself and come down from the cross, which would have meant abandoning His whole mission and purpose in coming into the world. But after His Resurrection, Jesus was "caught up to God and to His throne" in the event we know as "the Ascension." Thus, He Who was helpless on the cross is rewarded with the power to defeat Satan at last.

It may seem a bit strange to think of Jesus as this Child of the Church, since He is Lord of the Church. But what you must realize is that the biblical view of God's Church in not limited to the New Testament Church. For John, and in Reformed doctrine, the Church includes all the faithful of Old Testament Israel, as well as all who have put their faith in the risen Lord. So this woman symbolizes the Church, which is first the Jewish Church, and, therefore, indeed the mother of the Christ, and then the universal Church, whose Redeemer Christ is. This is a very strong basis for our belief that the New Testament Church is both the fulfillment and continuation of the Old Testament Church. All of the faithful under both covenants are included in God's Kingdom and united in Jesus the Messiah, both those who trusted God's promises and were looking for the Messiah to come, and those who have trusted Him since He has come.

Now, because he sees that he has been unable to defeat the woman's child, the dragon seeks in his fury to storm the very citadel of heaven itself and take the throne of God by force. But he is defeated and cast out of heaven with all the other angels who follow him in his rebellion. The faithful angels of God rejoice in Satan's defeat and expulsion from heaven but voice the warning John is seeking to give to mankind that Satan continues to carry on his war against God by attacking the Church. His pursuit of the woman is symbolic of his attempt through persecution by non-Christian Jews to destroy the Church in Palestine before it could spread any further.

Satan is thwarted in his attempt to destroy the Church as a whole in Palestine because Jewish Christians fleeing this persecution carry the Gospel to other lands. Eventually, the Gospel grows greatly among the gentiles, no longer confined to one place or to one ethnicity of people. Thus the dragon finds that the woman has been helped by the Lord to escape into "the wilderness," that is, anywhere outside Palestine, having been given "the two wings of the great eagle," which recalls the words of Isaiah 40:31, that those who wait upon Yahweh "shall mount up with wings like eagles." Thus, the Church escapes confinement and total annihilation by the evangelism of those fleeing the Sanhedrin. As has been repeated throughout history, Satan's efforts to suppress the Church through human persecution have backfired.

Because Satan has failed twice in his attempts to destroy God's work, first by a direct attack upon Jesus, and second by a direct attack upon the mother Church in Jerusalem, John warns his readers that, in his rage, Satan does not give up on the struggle. He cleverly begins a new campaign in which he does not attack the whole Church at once, but rather attacks "the rest of her offspring." Satan makes various attacks upon individual Christians, or particular groups of Christians, and mounts these attacks through unexpected agents. John ends this chapter with an ominous hint at what he is going to declare in the next chapter. For, at the end of this chapter, we see that Satan, preparing his next offensive against the Church, is standing on the sand of the sea. In apocalyptic literature, the sea is often a symbol of the arena of human government. Thus, John gives us an omen that the political realm, usually expected to provide protection for religion, will be the unexpected source or channel of Satan's continuing warfare against the Church. In my next chapter, I shall offer a fuller consideration of the implications of this cunning strategy and how Satan has employed it in the past and continues to do so.

But for the moment, let me take stock of what we find in this chapter, and summarize it like this. In this chapter, the conflict revealed as taking place in heaven between the Adversary and God's heavenly army sets the stage for what is occurring on earth. Satan, the Adversary, having sought and failed to destroy Christ, makes war on the rest of the children of the Church, in an attempt to destroy her, and thus salvage some kind of victory over Christ by making Him a King without a Kingdom. This is what this whole book is about, the warfare of Satan against God and His children and how the results of that warfare emerge in human events. But it is ultimately the story of the final victory of Christ and those who are faithful to Him.

In this story, John uses a lot of allegorical imagery, as I have said, to describe realities which it was not safe for him to identify literally. But it needs to be pointed out from this passage and others in this book that the Adversary whom John described in such allegorical terms as "a great red dragon" was nevertheless understood by John very seriously to be a personal reality. John had no question of the actual existence and intentions of Satan, though his description of Satan's appearance here is purely symbolic. In his writing of this book, John definitely intended to warn his readers, as Paul did in Ephesians 6, to "Put on the whole armor of God, that you may be able to stand against the wiles of the devil. For we wrestle not against flesh and blood, but against principalities, against powers, against the rulers of the darkness of this world, against spiritual wickedness in high places." John offers in this book a warning that wherever political evil threatens the Church or seeks to tame us to its will rather than God's, Satan is behind it, bringing his war with God to us, God's people.

However, John also intends to assure the Church in Asia that their suffering will not be long, from the perspective of eternity, and to encourage them faithfully and patiently to endure in the confident faith expressed in one of my favorite hymns that, "though the wrong seems oft' so strong, God is the ruler yet." The Church today has no less need of this assurance than did the Asian Church.

Now, you may say, "That's all very fine and good, but I just don't know about all this talk about Satan as an actual person. Surely, you're not saying that I have to believe in the actual existence of Satan in order to be a Christian, are you?" To which I must reply that "No, I am not saying that." I believe in the actual existence of Satan myself because of what I am convinced the Bible teaches us about him and because I have experienced his presence at times. But you don't have to believe he exists in order to be a true Christian. On the contrary, I am certain that all you have to believe to be saved is that you are a sinner, utterly lost and completely without hope apart from God's grace, and that Jesus of Nazareth is indeed the Son of God, that He died for your sin, and rose bodily from the grave, and that He is your Lord and Savior, seated at the right hand of the Father, present in His Church through the Holy Spirit, and coming again in glory to judge all people and establish His eternal Kingdom.

But for the sake of discussion, consider the fact that if Satan does exist and is actively engaged in such a campaign against the Church, it will be much easier for him to do his damage to the Church if we are unaware of his existence and therefore fail to be vigilant. He has had much more success with the clever tactic of attacking in an unexpected way, and what is more unexpected than trouble from someone you do not even believe exists? It is worth considering that just as surely as our scientific outlook on things causes many to say that there is no such person as Satan, it is the same outlook which causes so many to say that there is no God. If we can't touch it, see it, hear, smell, or taste it, or put it in a test tube, or measure it in some way, we say it isn't real. But that is a very dangerous assumption.

In the case of the reality of God, we say that even though we can't see Him, we see what He does, like we see the effect of the wind. John is warning us that even though we can't see Satan, we need to be alert and on our guard and recognize what he is doing, as well. If you go through the rest of your life still not believing that Satan is real, it will not mean that, just because you don't believe that, you are lost. But I ask you to think seriously about it for one reason. Regardless of whether you accept the reality of Satan, the Church and Christian values are under very energetic attack today from very subtle and unexpected sources. The forces of evil with which the Church must reckon today are of a very Satanic nature, even if you only consider Satan to be a symbol of evil. The Church is in great need of careful scrutiny of the motivations and directions of many in the world today, who have reason to exult over the decline of the Church's influence in the world. That decline, in and of itself, has caused many to fall away. But the Church that will triumph is the Church that faces all of the forces of Satan, or of people who serve well to stand in his place, with open eyes and enlightened minds and unswerving allegiance to and faith in the victorious Christ Who is our Lord.

I believe that it is extremely important for the Church to be aware of Satan's existence and activity and to resist him in every way, with confidence in the ultimate victory that is ours in Jesus Christ. We ignore the spiritual warfare in which we are entangled to our own peril. There are in our day, as there were in John's day, people in positions of great political power who desire to destroy the Church and all for which it stands, though they try to appear objective and tolerant. Both the warning and the assurance John shared with his original readers apply to the Church in all ages. Satan is at war with our God and, therefore, with us. We must be always on our guard and stand up to oppose him where we find him. While it would be irresponsible to claim that Satan is behind every little thing we personally do not like, we still need to exercise prayerful and careful discernment of Satan's activity hiding behind the anti-Christian agenda of many today, who put on the masquerade of neutrality, both within and outside the visible Church. And, by the way, according to the Bible, Jesus certainly believed in and experienced the reality of Satan. After all, He created Satan. Satan rebelled against Him. He has conquered Satan and wants to share that victory with us.

CHAPTER 9

In the Image of Satan
(Revelation 13:1–18)

At the end of chapter 12, the great red dragon, which symbolizes Satan, is pictured by John as standing on the sand of the sea. Here, we find a beast rising out of the sea and resembling the dragon in that, like the dragon, it also has seven heads and ten horns. This beast, then, is made in the image of Satan. The fact that it rises from the sea means that it represents some evil arising from the realm of human government. Although John has previously presented the dragon as having seven heads and ten horns, the real significance of these heads and horns pertains to the nature of the beast created in Satan's image, rather than to Satan himself. The meaning of these seven heads and ten horns will be explained when we deal with chapter 17 of the Apocalypse. For the moment, let it suffice to say that the seven heads and ten horns of the beast are apocalyptic signs which clearly indicate that this beast represents none other than the Roman Empire and its emperors, culminating in Domitian. More will be explained about that later.

The "blasphemous name" upon the seven heads of this beast refers to the claim that these emperors were gods. This claim, with the troubles which befell the Church in John's time because of it, is the occasion for the writing of the Apocalypse. It is through this claim of divinity for the Roman emperors that John sees Satan putting into effect his plan for attacking the Church through an unexpected source.

It had always been the policy of Rome, unlike previous conquerors, to allow their captured subjects complete religious freedom. They had not forced their own religion upon any of the nations they had conquered, and had not interfered with the people's free exercise of their particular religions. In fact, the Romans were more inclined to incorporate aspects of the religions of other peoples into their own. The Romans had established a lasting peace and security for all who had come under their rule, and their policy of religious tolerance had proven to be a wise policy in that it eliminated what would have otherwise been a major reason for those peoples to rebel. The vast majority of the subjects of Rome, including Paul and other early Christians, were grateful for the peace, security and religious freedom they had enjoyed, and gladly learned to live as subjects of Rome because of these things. Christians, such as Paul and Peter, had no quarrel with Rome in the beginning because for the first thirty years of the Christian Church's existence, the Church was included in Rome's protection of religious freedom. Even Jesus had commanded that Roman rule should be respected, though considered subordinate to God's rule, when He said, "Render unto Caesar the things that are Caesar's, and unto God the things that are God's" (Matthew 22:21).

So what went wrong? Why did John find it necessary at the end of the First Century AD to condemn Rome as Satan's agent for persecution of the Church when just thirty-five or so years earlier, Rome had been as much the protector of the Church as of any other religious group?

The answer to this question begins with events that took place a few decades before the birth of Jesus. After Octavian became the first emperor of Rome, assuming the name Caesar Augustus, the pagan people of the province of Asia insisted upon worshiping him as a god, as it was their custom to worship their kings in this way. Augustus was personally opposed to the idea, but in order to keep them happy, he allowed them to worship him. However, because he considered the idea repugnant and beneath the dignity of Romans, he only allowed this practice to be continued as customary in the province of Asia. He refused to allow himself to be worshiped in Rome. He also allowed the Jews in Asia, or anywhere else, for that matter, to be exempt from any requirement to worship him, or any god but their own, the living and true God. Thus, Augustus intended to continue the Roman policy of noninterference and protection of religious freedom in the several provinces.

In spite of the good intentions of Augustus, without meaning to do so, he had opened the door for a corruption which would prove disastrous to Christians. For after the death of Augustus, the Senate of Rome did what he would not allow them to do during his life. They declared him a god. It became customary from that time that when the emperor died, he would be declared a god. For a time, although this was offensive to Jews and Christians and some others, it was basically harmless in terms of causing any real trouble between the Church and the empire.

Meanwhile, gentile Christians in the province of Asia began to experience persecution from their pagan neighbors in the form of pressure to take part in the emperor cult as a sign of Asia's allegiance to Rome. Jewish Christians were not exposed to such pressure because of the exemption which Augustus had granted to the Jews. But the pagan Asians insisted that gentile Christians in Asia had no such exemption, and should, therefore, conform to the Asian custom.

At first, the pressure which was imposed upon the Christians was merely a sort of ostracism. Pagan Asians began to treat Asian Christians who refused to worship the emperor as bad citizens. They began to abandon friendships and business dealings with Christians. At first, this was all they could do, because their Roman overlords would not tolerate any disturbance of the peace or acts of violence to persuade the Christians to conform to the accepted practice of their pagan culture. Early on, Rome simply had no interest in forcing anyone to participate in worshiping the emperor. So the pressure the pagans put on the Christians was more of a nuisance than an actual threat in the beginning.

The first hint of real trouble came when the emperor Caligula, also known as Gaius, the third Roman emperor, became the first emperor to take the idea of the divinity of the emperor seriously.

Whereas Augustus had detested the idea, and Tiberius had been content to remain a mortal until his death, Caligula felt that being a god would do little good for his reign as emperor after he was dead. He accordingly coerced the Roman Senate to declare him a god shortly after he became emperor. Caligula did not directly attack the Church for its refusal to worship him, because every province cooperated with his command that he be worshiped with a statue of himself being erected in every capital city, and the Christians had no voice in these decisions. The one exception was the province of Judea, which refused to comply with this order. Caligula would have reduced Jerusalem to ruins for this refusal, but he was killed by his own bodyguards before the order to do so could be carried out. His statue only made it as far as the steps of the Jerusalem Temple before his death, and not into the Holy of Holies, which would have brought on the Jewish Rebellion many years sooner than it actually occurred. Even though Caligula thus troubled the Jews, and not the Church, over the issue of emperor worship, his disregard even for the exemption that Augustus had granted to the Jews was an encouragement to the pagan Asians to increase their pressure upon Asian Christians to conform.

Caligula was followed by Claudius, who represented the return of some sanity to the throne of the empire. He was not declared a god until after his death, and did not encourage the harassment of the Asian Christians in any way. He even plainly stated that he was not a god and was not likely to become one.

However, after Claudius came Nero. Nero was the fifth Roman emperor, and the second to have himself declared a god during his life. He was the first Roman emperor to persecute Christians. His persecution, however, was limited to Christians in the general vicinity of Rome. He required everyone to refer to him as "lord and god." The Christians in Rome refused to do so. Presumably, this was at least part of the reason why he chose to accuse Christians of the burning of Rome, for which he himself is said to have been responsible. He hated Christians so much for their refusal to worship him that he even declared it unlawful to be a Christian. He tortured and killed many Christians in Rome. Tradition has it that he ordered the executions of Paul and Peter. While he did not pursue the Christians to the extent of seeking them out in the provinces, the actions he did take naturally encouraged a growing mistreatment of Christians in the province of Asia. He was particularly fond of tying Christians to poles, dowsing them with oil, and setting them on fire to light his garden parties.

After Nero's death, civil war erupted in Rome. In the space of one year, three different men were proclaimed emperor, each being deposed by the next, and none reigning long enough to be taken seriously as emperor, so that John does not even count them in his numbering of the emperors. Their names were Galba, Otho and Vitellius. The third of these was finally deposed by Vespasian, the sixth undisputed emperor of Rome. He returned from the war against the Jews at the request of the Senate to become emperor.

Vespasian represented a return to the former Roman sensibility. He did not care for the deification of himself and found no cause for religious persecution. Even after he and his son, Titus, put down the Jewish Rebellion, which took place in 66–70 AD, Vespasian was very lenient in his punishment of Judea, compared with what could have been expected from most dictators. His son, Titus, who succeeded him as the seventh Roman emperor, followed Vespasian's example, and ruled the empire well and fairly for the brief two years of his reign, although he did destroy the city of Jerusalem and the Temple in putting down the rebellion.

Titus was succeeded as emperor by his brother, Domitian, who it is said, poisoned Titus in order to become the eighth Roman emperor (not counting Galba, Otho and Vitellius). In John's view, the reign of Domitian was the full harvest of the corrupt seed that had been planted very craftily by Satan when Augustus first allowed himself to be worshiped in the province of Asia. Domitian was the first Roman emperor to take the idea of his own divinity so seriously that he enacted an official policy that not only required everyone to worship him, but also forbade anyone to address him at any time in any way other than to call him "our lord and our god." He believed himself to be the incarnation of the Greco-Roman god Zeus, or Jupiter. The worship of the emperor which previous emperors had merely allowed in Asia, Domitian made mandatory throughout the empire.

As the result of his policies, gentile Christians in Asia who had already been subject to ostracism and financial difficulties were now subject to torture and execution if they refused to worship Domitian by going to one of the temples of the emperor cult, casting a pinch of incense on the altar fire, and proclaiming, "Caesar is lord." To non-Christians, this seemed like such a simple thing to do. It was not just a religious act. It was like saluting the flag or standing with hand over heart during the singing of "The Star-Spangled Banner" in our culture. Failure to comply with this custom was seen by the community as unpatriotic, or even an act of treason against the emperor. It seemed like so little to ask in the eyes of the non-Christians in Asia. Yet, to a true Christian, it was impossible to comply with this requirement because for a true Christian, only Jesus is Lord.

Thus, in Domitian, the reversal of Roman religious tolerance was complete. Rome, which had once forbidden religious persecution, now became the source of a vicious campaign to destroy the Christian Church unless the Christians would acknowledge Domitian as lord instead of Jesus. As John saw it, this was how Satan cleverly carried on his own war against Christ and His Church, causing persecution to come from Rome, which would normally have been expected to protect the people's religious freedom.

It was because of this that the Church came to have a much different opinion of Rome than that which Paul had expressed. At the beginning of the Church, Paul and some others had seen Rome as the unwitting agent of God to preserve the peace so that the Church could evangelize and flourish. But by the end of the century, the change in the policies of Rome caused John and others to condemn the empire as a collaborator with Satan, a beast made in the image of Satan, arising out of the "sea" of human government to make war on the Lord and His Church. John asserts that the power of the Roman Empire is the delegated power of Satan himself. To worship the emperor was, therefore, to worship Satan through him. It would amount to treason against Christ our King, as well as blasphemy.

John is warning Asian Christians that the persecutions they have been suffering are about to become worse. Their enemy is the mighty Roman Empire, the most irresistible earthly force of that day and time. He describes this enemy as a beast far more dreadful than any previous kingdom or empire. It has the swift attack of a leopard, the brute force of a bear, and the regal splendor, the power, and fearsome voice of a lion. John warns them that, confronted by such an enemy as this, which bears the image of Satan their great enemy, it is inevitable that the Christians who are faithful to Jesus are going to suffer, many even being executed. Yet, he assures them that the time of Rome's power will be short-lived, and tells them that such dreadful circumstances call for the saints to respond with "endurance and faith." They must refuse to call anyone but Jesus their Lord. They must accept even death as a consequence, in the faith that when He returns, Christ will vindicate those who are faithful to Him. Domitian, as head of this perverted Rome, embodies the full presence of this great and terrible beast that Rome has become, but they are not to bow down to him or worship him.

There is another beast in this vision, a beast which arises out of the earth. This beast represents the Asian priests of the emperor cult. It, too, is in the image of Satan, for it "spoke like a dragon." The meaning of this beast is that now the pagan Asian priests have what they have wanted for nearly three quarters of a century: the authority of the Roman Empire to force their Christian neighbors to worship the emperor. They have been given authority from the emperor to deprive anyone who does not worship him of the right to free commerce and even of their lives. Christians who refused to call Domitian lord, and thus failed to receive on their hand or forehead the mark that was placed upon worshipers as they entered the temple of the emperor cult, would at least be denied the right to make a living, and might even be executed. This mark is described as "the name of the beast or the number of its name." The numerical value of the letters in the name of the beast is said to add up to 666.

The number 666 is the symbol for spiritual evil and imperfection, the total opposite of God and His holiness. It is interesting that this number, by which John refers to Domitian, is the numerical equivalent of the name Nero Caesar, written in Hebrew letters. This will be explained in a later chapter. The significance of the number itself is that 6 is not just one less than 7; it is the opposite of 7. Six is separated from seven by the whole number, 1. It is thus wholly unholy. Three 6s, then, stands for complete spiritual unholiness. The beast, which represents the emperor who claims to be God, is to be ridiculed for this claim, because John is saying that not only is the emperor not God, he is in every way totally the opposite of God.

What John describes here is an alliance between corrupt government and false religion. He declares that it is inevitable that when there is such an alliance, God's people will be called upon by that alliance to go along with things that are atrocious to God, and will suffer at the hands of that alliance if they refuse. A modern example is the imprisonment of Christians who have blocked access to so-called "clinics" to prevent the exploitation of women and the slaughter of unborn babies by abortion. But John is insisting that we must not compromise our allegiance to Jesus Christ for fear of persecution. It is very unlikely that when such an unholy alliance arises, the Church will be able to do anything to stop it. But John is telling the Asian Christians, and we need to hear it, too, that such circumstances do not excuse Christians complying with things which offend God. Such events call for the patient endurance and faithfulness of God's saints to remain loyal to Jesus Christ and stand up for His truth, despite the consequences.

This situation is not limited to John's day. It is a recurring evil. Napoleon was crowned emperor by Pope Pius VII. Hitler was supported by the so-called "Nazi Christians" who took over the national German Church. We never know when another such unholy alliance will emerge to trouble the true people of God. It seems to be occurring in America today, as secular humanism is more and more forced upon us by a government that has forgotten its foundation. What we need to learn from John is that these situations are occasions for the Church to remain faithful in word and deed, no matter what the consequences, and endure the trouble we must face with patience because all such alliances inevitably fall and the day is coming when Christ will put an end to them forever. In such times, we may feel torn between patriotism and our Faith. But the choice is clear for the true Christian. Our allegiance to Christ must supersede all others.

A minor point yet worth noting is that verse 15, "And it was allowed to give breath to the image of the beast so that the image of the beast should even speak," probably refers to the emperor's statue being fitted with a movable jaw, like a ventriloquist's dummy, so that it could be made to appear to speak. Perhaps a priest of the cult would hide behind the statue and "speak" through it. Perhaps the priests of the cult actually practiced ventriloquism, "throwing one's voice," and thus "giving breath to the image of the beast." This is just speculation on my part. In any event, John is accusing the priests of the emperor cult of intentionally using fraudulent means to keep the people fooled. It is as much as to say that they are not just sincere but misguided worshipers of the emperor, but willing perpetrators of a great hoax, of which they themselves are fully aware. It may well be for us to consider how many of the leaders of other religions, who reject the Lordship of Jesus, probably do not really even believe their own teachings, but are simply using false religion as a way to gain wealth and power by deceiving gullible people. Also, how many false teachers are there in the visible Church who are charlatans, making grandiose claims for themselves to attract a following for themselves rather than for Jesus? How many other false teachers are there in the visible Church who teach unbiblical ideas such as universalism, who entered ordained ministry for motives other than building the Kingdom of Jesus Christ? May God give us wisdom to discern what religious expression is genuine or counterfeit among preachers and politicians who pretend to belong to our Lord Jesus while advancing the goals of the Adversary.

CHAPTER IO

A Call to Endurance
(Revelation 14:1–20)

Mount Zion was the hill in Jerusalem on which the Temple of Yahweh stood. It is thus the symbol of the true worship of the one true and living God, and of His just rule and judgment of the affairs of men and nations. Isaiah and Micah, and possibly some other prophet whose words they gave a renewed emphasis, had prophesied that, "It shall come to pass in the latter days that the mountain of the house of Yahweh shall be established as the highest of the mountains, and shall be raised above the hills; and all nations shall flow to it…For out of Zion shall go forth the law, and the word of Yahweh from Jerusalem" (Isaiah 2:2–3, Micah 4:1–2). The city of Jerusalem was that place "where Yahweh God had chosen for His name to dwell." Because of Mount Zion, the city itself is sometimes referred to as Zion. It was understood to be the seat of God's presence and government upon the earth. The Messianic hopes of the Jews were inseparably bound to this city and this hill, from which they expected and hoped for the Messiah to reign supreme over all the earth.

John has just given us the description of the beast rising from the sea, created in the image of Satan, and representing the Roman Empire, and the beast rising from the earth, masquerading as a lamb, but speaking like a devil, enforcing the worship of the first beast, and thus representing the false priests of the emperor cult. Having made

75

clear the threat that faces the people of God and the source of their troubles, John now presents to us a more encouraging portion of his vision, in which at last, Jesus the Messiah appears upon Mount Zion as the Lamb of God. The clear meaning here is that Jesus, Who was led like a lamb to be slaughtered as a sacrifice for our sin, comes again to judge and to rule the earth. How wonderful it is to know that the One Who is to judge and lead and govern us through all eternity as the sheep of God is the very One Who, as the Lamb of God, has become one of us, so that His understanding of us—of our needs and of our fears—is perfect, for He became like us in every way, except that He did not sin.

With the Lamb, there are 144,000 who have His name and His Father's name written on their foreheads. These are singing a new song before God. It is the song of redemption, which only they are able to learn. The number here, of course, is not a literal figure. It is only a symbolic number, intended to state that the full number of the redeemed are with Christ. That is to say, there is no one who is redeemed who does not stand with Christ, and none of those who stand with Christ will be missing when He comes to claim His throne and execute judgment upon the ungodly.

When John speaks of these as being "chaste" or "virgins" who "have not defiled themselves with women," he is not advocating celibacy as opposed to marriage. What he is saying is that these have not given in to the pressure exerted upon them to participate in false worship. Much of the false and idolatrous worship of the ancient world involved ritual prostitution. Because of this, it had become standard symbolism among the prophets to refer to any form of false worship as "playing the harlot," even if that particular false worship did not actually involve temple prostitutes. Since the problem that John is addressing is one of an attempt to force false worship upon the people of God, he refers to those who do not give in as virgins, who have kept themselves undefiled before God and have not prostituted themselves by participating in the worship of the emperor.

Next in John's vision, there is an angel sent out to proclaim the twofold message of the Gospel of salvation and the coming of God's judgment. There seem to be a lot of people in our day who do not feel that the message of forgiveness and peace is compatible with the message of the wrath to come. But the two are actually inseparable. Holiness cannot abide or tolerate wickedness. Judgment is necessary because God is holy. He would prove Himself unjust if He did not destroy the unrepentant. But the good news of the Gospel of Christ is that God does what is not necessary. He provides the way of forgiveness out of His free and unmerited grace toward us. He chooses to do this because He loves us and does not want to enact the just punishment which must fall upon us if we do not repent. It is thus the very God Who is our Judge Who reaches out to us in Jesus Christ to offer us deliverance from the death sentence He Himself must impose upon sinful humanity.

In this vision, there is a second angel, who echoes the words of Isaiah, "Fallen, fallen is Babylon the great" (Isaiah 21:9). In this instance, however, "Babylon" is a symbolic reference to Rome, "who made all nations drink the wine of her impure passion." This is a declaration of the impending doom of Rome and her empire because it had promoted and enforced the religious harlotry of turning away from the one true and living God to worship the emperor.

A third angel appears and pronounces judgment upon all who cooperate and participate in the emperor cult. Here is the central warning and concern of this book, as it were in a nutshell. Faced with the difficult choice of either participating in the worship of the emperor, even superficially, in order to save one's life and livelihood, or faithfully refusing to call anyone but Jesus Lord, and thus risking persecution and death, some of the people in the churches of Asia were saying to themselves and others, "Why not go along with this, and attend the worship of the emperor, just for the sake of appearances, just to show we are loyal citizens? As long as we know that Jesus is Lord, why not pacify our neighbors by giving the outward appearance of allegiance to the emperor as a god? We can do that publicly, so as not to offend anybody, but privately, we shall worship only Jesus." In this book, John is definite and emphatic as he replies, "Oh no, you can't!" Our allegiance to Christ must be complete and absolute. We must avoid even the appearance of evil. (I Thessalonians 5:22) We must not compromise with the servants of Satan. We cannot be publicly pagan and privately Christian, nor publicly Christian and privately pagan. It must be all or nothing. Jesus did not die privately for us. He died publicly, mocked and scorned by the mob. We cannot call Him our only Lord privately, and yet acknowledge another lord publicly, and have any place in His Kingdom. Our exclusive allegiance to Him must be complete, both in public and in private. If we are not willing to bear the shame and hatred of the world with Him, we shall not share in His victory over the world, either. Damnation will overtake any who deny Jesus to save themselves in this world, even if they are nominal members of the visible Church.

In addition, we are called by Christ to make others His disciples. How are we to bring others to a saving relationship with Him as their only Lord and Savior, if we do not insist upon honoring His exclusive claim upon our own lives? If we allow anything or anyone else to share an equal place with Jesus in our lives, why should others bother about Him on the basis of such a weak witness as that?

John says, "Here is a call for the endurance of the saints, those who keep the commandments of God and the faith of Jesus." This is a break from what would normally be expected of a Jewish apocalyptic writer at this point. He has just been proclaiming the coming judgment of God upon Rome, with the Messiah returning to rule and to judge from Mount Zion, and the damnation of those who are unfaithful along with the pagans. It would be expected at this point that there would be a call to arms. But instead of urging the people of God to rally for an armed offensive against the enemies of God and His Church, John issues a call for endurance. What can this mean?

It does not mean that we are not involved in spiritual warfare. It does not mean that we are not to fight against what is evil. It does mean, however, that we fight in a different way than those who take up the sword. In the midst of a sinful world which demands that we give our loyalty and devotion to something or someone less than Jesus, we defeat the evil around us, not by violence, but merely by pointing evil out for what it is and refusing to give in to it. Even if refusing to give in means that we die, yet we are the victors in Christ. If we even go so far as to lay down our lives in loyalty to Jesus, it means that we have not allowed even our very lives to take first place in our hearts ahead of Jesus, and the evil has not been able to separate us from Him. It was so in the days of John, when the Church was persecuted by Rome, and John declared the word he received in this vision, "Blessed are the dead who die in the Lord." It is so today, whenever Christians, in loyalty to Christ, stand up for what is right, regardless of what it may cost them. The preacher who will not speak the truth for fear of losing his job is not worth the wood in his pulpit. And no other church member is any less responsible before God to stand up for what is right in His sight. We are called and chosen and commissioned by Christ to do this, no matter how much you may be accused of being narrow-minded in a world of sinners who are "broad-minded" enough for everything but the Word of God.

Jesus is pictured as being seated upon a white cloud, a symbol of victorious judgment, and reaping the harvest of the earth with a sharp sickle. This calls to mind Jesus' own parable of the wheat and the tares. We are reminded what it means to endure in the name of Christ in a world filled with those who are openly hostile to Him and with those who appear to be his disciples but are not. We cannot separate the world clearly enough always to distinguish who belongs to which category, who is a genuine disciple and who is not. It falls to us simply to remain faithful and to endure, confident that Jesus will, as in that parable, separate the wheat from the tares in the last judgment.

An angel appears to assist the Lord in reaping the earth as Jesus had indicated in His teaching. The terror of the judgment that is coming upon those who resist the Lord's Anointed is indicated by the symbolism of the treading of the grapes of wrath in the "great winepress of the wrath of God," from which the blood of the wicked flows "as high as a horse's bridle" for about two hundred miles. It is very significant that this destruction of the wicked is said to occur "outside the city." You will recall that when Jesus, the Messiah, the Holy One of Israel, who should have sat upon the throne of David, was crucified, it was done outside the city. Jesus was cast out of the city in which it was His birthright to reign as the King of the Jews. He was shamefully put to death outside the city—His city! John is saying that when Jesus appears upon Mount Zion to claim His Kingdom, it will be the wicked who will be cast out of the Holy City and utterly destroyed.

In the meantime, there is still the ongoing struggle of the evil against Christ and His Church. The struggle goes on in many different forms. There are those who openly deny Christ and assault the Church from outside. There are those who feign impartiality, but work devotedly against everything for which the true Church stands. There are those who claim to be His disciples, but contradict or water down the Scriptures. There is turmoil and tribulation for the faithful on many fronts. And there is still and always a call to endurance. Our trials are great, but our redemption and vindication are drawing nigh with Jesus, our Righteous Judge.

There are those in the Church today who would have us pacify the enemies of Christ, just as John had to deal with those in the Church in Asia who were urging their fellow members to appease the emperor cult. These modern apostates would have us deny the Word of God when it condemns homosexuality. They would have us defile the Sacraments of God by acts which deny their sacredness. They do not set up any concrete idols, of course, but they would have us worship the nation or the government or the god of popular opinion by letting the pronouncements of these take the place of Christ and His Word in establishing Church policy, even to the point of supporting the worship of Satan through modern false gods of convenience, career and libertinism by the child sacrifice of unfettered abortion. Let those who are faithful still be faithful, and endure these awful days. But let us do so by waging spiritual warfare through words and lives of faithfulness, as Christ commands.

Those who are faithful in the Church must speak out against the evils of our society and of our world. We must speak and act in accordance with the Word of God. We must stand fast in His truth, though multitudes oppose and slander us, both within and without the Church. But we must do so without violence. We must declare what is right and denounce what is wrong, but do no harm to anyone, even though they might do harm to us. That is the way of Christ, Who allowed sinners to nail Him to the cross. God's judgment upon the wicked is coming. That is not in the Church's hands.

Now is the time of grace and warning. Let those who are faithful to Jesus Christ endure whatever the struggle may cost us in whatever area we must struggle for peace, righteousness and justice. But let us do so in peaceful and loving ways, not gloating over the victory that is sure in Christ, but with broken hearts, desperately yearning over those who do not see that the judgment is coming.

Of course, that does not mean that if some criminal comes into a church service or a school housed in a church building, and attacks us, we do not have the right to defend ourselves and each other from such an attack. Jesus even said, "But now let the one who has a moneybag take it, and likewise a knapsack. And let the one who has no sword sell his cloak and buy one" (Luke 22:36). Thus He confirmed our right to self-defense in such cases. However, He intends for us to keep the peace as good citizens as far as it depends on us. He does not authorize us to resist arrest if the government outlaws Christianity, but He calls on us to endure it peacefully and simply refuse to abandon our witness if we are arrested and put on trial for it, seeking to persuade our persecutors peacefully.

This is part of what Jesus was talking about when He said, "blessed are they that mourn, for they shall be comforted." In addition to our personal experiences of loss which bring us grief, there is also cause to mourn over a lost world. Christ has come because in God's grief over His lost creation, He determined that He would not allow Himself to be bereaved of us all. Christ came to restore those who would accept Him. There is great joy to be known in the salvation Jesus offers. But it is joy that can be had only beyond the suffering of God's grief over our sinfulness. We can't appreciate or appropriate the Good News until we know the bad news. Only those who care about the condition of the world in relation to God enough to share His grief over our sin, and commit themselves to the Gospel of Christ as the remedy, will ever know the joy of His Kingdom. We must "keep our eyes on the prize and hold on."

CHAPTER II

The Wrath of God
(Revelation 15:1–16:21)

In chapter 14, John declared that whoever worshiped the beast or received its mark would also "drink the wine of God's wrath, poured unmixed into the cup of His anger." Now he proceeds to announce the final outpouring of the wrath of God that is going to come upon the Roman Empire. The grapes of the earth's iniquity having been reaped and trodden in the "great winepress of the wrath of God," the beast and its followers, John says, are going to suffer the bitter fruit of their own iniquity. He describes this final reckoning as coming in the form of the seven last plagues, with which "the wrath of God is ended." Now, the word that is translated "ended" there also means "fulfilled" or "completed." I believe that one of these latter possible renderings of the word would be more accurate, as will be clarified later.

As soon as the seven angels who bear the seven last plagues appear, John is shown a scene that is symbolic of the security of the faithful. He sees those who are faithful to Jesus Christ, standing along the edge of a glassy sea, singing the praises of God. They stand there in safety to behold the destruction of God's enemies. It is reminiscent, as it is meant to be, of the children of Israel standing by the shore of the Red Sea and witnessing the overthrow of Pharaoh's army. These are delivered from the destruction of the wicked, just as the Israelites were delivered from the destruction that befell the Egyptians. As the Israelites crossed the Red Sea safely, these have crossed the sea of death into eternal life. They are safe in Jesus Christ, and shall merely behold the outpouring of the wrath of God. It will not come near them. They sing "the song of Moses…and the song of the Lamb," which is a song of rejoicing in the justice of the one true and living God Who delivered the Israelites through Moses, and delivers His Church by the blood of Jesus, while bringing disaster upon the unrepentant.

After John is thus assured of the security of God's people, even in a time of great calamity, his attention is turned to the heavenly temple. He calls it "the temple of the tent of witness." There is a close connection between this word for "witness" and our English word "martyr." In a sense, this heavenly temple is meant to be understood as the dwelling place of the martyrs of the Faith. But the witnesses who have been martyred for their faith, who stand by the sea of glass, have not yet entered into this heavenly temple. It is the heavenly prototype for the Jerusalem Temple which replaced the tabernacle that Moses erected in the wilderness, and thus is related also to that tent of meeting. The seven angels who come out of the temple are "robed in pure bright linen, and their breasts girded with golden girdles." That is to say, they are dressed as the priests of God. Each of these priestly angels is given a bowl filled with the wrath of the ever-living God. They are here assigned as the priests of His vengeance. They come forth from the temple of the tent of witness to execute the wrath of God upon the wicked. John says that the glory of God fills the temple with smoke so that no one may enter until the seven plagues of the angels are ended. This is reminiscent of when the glory of God filled the tabernacle in the wilderness with a cloud, and Moses and the people could not enter it. Even the redeemed may not enter that heavenly temple until the corruption of man's wickedness is fully consumed in God's wrath.

The plagues that are unleashed upon the Roman Empire, and thus symbolically upon all the wicked of the world, are basically those which were rained down upon Pharaoh and his people. There are "foul and evil sores," just as the Egyptians were plagued with boils and sores. There are plagues by which the sea, the rivers and the fountains of water are turned into blood, just as the Nile River and all the water in Egypt was turned to blood. There is a plague of darkness, like Egypt also suffered. There is a plague of enormous hail, even greater than the hail that fell upon Egypt. The plague of fierce heat is one which does not appear in the story of Moses and Pharaoh, but it is related, in a way, to the plague of darkness, in that God has the power even to move the sun to such opposite extremes. All of these plagues which are related to the plagues on Egypt are meant to show that the God Who is known in Jesus Christ is the same God Who punished Egypt and delivered the Israelites. That very same God, Who rules all creation, is the One Who will destroy the wicked world of the Roman Empire and deliver the disciples of the Lord Jesus.

Also reminiscent of the story of the Exodus is the drying up of the river Euphrates, but there is a difference. In Exodus, the Red Sea was parted, and the sea bottom became a path of dry land for the Hebrews to leave Egypt. Here, the Euphrates is dried up to allow "the kings from the east" to enter the territory of the Roman Empire. Since the Euphrates formed the border between the Roman Empire and the land of the Parthians, this strongly suggests that part of the judgment of God against the Romans would include what they feared most, an invasion by the Parthian hordes. As if in response to this threat, the dragon, the beast and the false prophet send forth "three foul spirits like frogs…who go abroad to the kings of the whole world, to assemble them for battle." That these demonic spirits appear in the form of frogs seems to be a reference to the counterfeit religion of the beast, still trying to convince everyone that he is God. They even spring forth from the evil, mock trinity of the dragon, the beast and the false prophet, who are the evil contrast to the goodness of Father, Son and Holy Spirit, as the emperor tries to usurp the place of God. It is like the magicians of Pharaoh trying to duplicate the signs Yahweh worked through Moses in Egypt. They could counterfeit some of them, but their power was overshadowed by Yahweh's so that they were inevitably beaten. Even so, John is telling the Asian Christians, the counterfeit religion of the emperor cult, though it fools so many people for a time, will eventually be shown up for the fraud it is. The emperor and his empire and his worshipers will not stand before the wrath of God when the great day of the true and living God comes.

The frog-like demons assemble the kings of the whole earth "at a place which is called in Hebrew *Armageddon*." What you have probably heard about this place, Armageddon, is that someday all the armies of the earth will converge upon one last great battlefield, and fight the final battle which will end all human history. But that simply is not what John is saying. He is talking about something quite different. Armageddon simply means "hill of Megiddo." There was no such hill that literally bore that name, although it might refer to the mound upon which the city of Megiddo was built. Below the hills that surround Megiddo, however, there is a vast plain called the Plain of Esdraelon. Megiddo stood at one entrance into this plain. This great plain was the scene of Israel's greatest battles. It has long been associated with great struggle and conflict, to the point that its very name is symbolic of the same. John uses its name here to draw on that symbolism. It was there that God gave victory to the Israelites over the army of the Canaanite general, Sisera. This place played an important role in the battles of Syria and Assyria against Samaria. It was on this plain that King Josiah of Judah, one of her most righteous kings, was defeated and killed by Pharaoh Neco of Egypt, which defeat began the great weakening of Judah that eventually led to their destruction by the Babylonians. The name "Armageddon" is thus symbolic of decisive battle.

But it is not a literal combat among human armies that John has in mind here. Rather, he is making symbolic reference to the most decisive victory of all time, that which Jesus Christ won in His battle with Satan on the cross. When John speaks of Armageddon, he has in mind, once again, the quotation from the prophecy of Zechariah mentioned earlier. "I will pour out on the house of David and the inhabitants of Jerusalem a spirit of compassion and supplication, so that, when they look on him whom they have pierced, they shall mourn for him, as one mourns for an only child, and weep bitterly over him, as one weeps over a first-born. On that day, the mourning in Jerusalem will be as great as the mourning for Hadadrimmon in the plain of Megiddo" (Zechariah 12:10–11).

Here is the connecting thread between John's account of the Gospel and Revelation that I mentioned in my introduction. John clearly relates this passage from Zechariah to the Crucifixion of our Lord Jesus in John 19:34, where he says that the piercing of Jesus' side with a Roman spear was to fulfill the Scripture that says, "They shall look on him whom they have pierced." Revelation 1:7 again refers to this prophecy of Zechariah, saying, "Behold, he is coming with the clouds, and every eye will see him, everyone who pierced him." Revelation 16:16 is a third reference to this same passage from Zechariah, which John clearly relates to the death of Jesus upon the cross. Given this fact of the relevance of the Zechariah passage to the Crucifixion, it is clear that the gathering of the armies of the wicked at Armageddon, the hill of Megiddo, is also for John related to the Crucifixion. It is the symbolic reference to the hill called Golgotha.

Armageddon is merely a symbol for decisive victory. John, having clearly connected the passage from Zechariah about Megiddo, and someone being pierced and looked upon by those who are gathered there, with the Crucifixion of Jesus, is not talking about Armageddon as a last great battle between the United States allied with Israel and the Soviet Union allied with the enemies of Israel, as so many have falsely taught. Rather, John is talking about the decisive battle between Jesus and Satan. The cross is Jesus' Armageddon. Golgotha is Jesus' hill of victory. All the armies of the earth that seek to destroy and dominate others are the armies of Satan in this passage, no matter from which nation they come. By laying down His life for the sake of sinners, rather than taking up arms and giving in to the evil of war and hatred, Jesus has defeated them all. They could not force Him to participate in their evil. Furthermore, John is declaring that there is a day coming when even the Jews who have rejected Jesus will look on Him whom they have pierced, realize the truth, finally see their Messiah, and mourn for Him as the Canaanites wailed for their young men who fell at Megiddo, especially in the village of Hadadrimmon, which was often caught up in these battles, and seems to have been named for the false god, Hadadrimmon. It is also where Josiah died, and is thus connected with the mourning of the Jews over him. The Jews wanted a Messiah who would slaughter their enemies. They wanted a sword-wielding savior. Jesus instead went to the hill of Golgotha to fight against the enemies of all mankind, hatred, our own sinfulness, Satan, and death, not by taking up the sword and joining in our struggle against each other, but by giving His own life for us all. He won the victory over all the forces around us and within us that threaten to destroy us all. He calls us to share His victory with friend and foe alike by the same self-denial.

Being "Him Whom they have pierced," Jesus, as we behold Him, is indeed God's "only child." He is God's "firstborn." He shall be seen someday, "coming with the clouds." He was mourned in Jerusalem, just as Josiah and many others were mourned on the Plain of Megiddo. Zechariah was indeed talking about Him. John understood this, and wanted us to know.

The cross is Jesus' Armageddon. The gathering of the armies of the world to do battle against Christ and His Church does not predict a specific point in time yet to come or a specific conflict between or among human armies some time off in the future. Rather, it symbolizes all of history, from beginning to end, as those who seek to conquer and oppress are always thereby rejecting the way and the Lordship of Christ, and are thus always at war with Him. Armageddon is not a future moment in time. It is all of human history, centered upon Christ's death on the cross. The two-part event of Christ's Crucifixion-Resurrection is His Armageddon, His decisive victory over the forces of evil for all time, and the focal point of all history.

The decisive battle has been won on the cross. Yet John knows that the war rages on. Satan refuses to admit defeat. Men still refuse to repent and acknowledge their true Lord. Therefore, a day of judgment must come. Babylon, by which John refers to Rome, the great conqueror, will be annihilated. John is saying that though Rome should assemble all the armies of all the kings of the earth, she cannot withstand the wrath of God that is coming upon her on account of the abominations of the emperor cult. He is saying that the day of

Rome's destruction will be a day of the Lord's vindication of Himself and of His saints.

In John's vision, when the wrath of God comes in the last cycle of plagues, it does not merely come to an end. It is complete. It is fulfilled. In the earlier cycles of plagues in this book, when the waters or the earth are smitten, the destruction was described as only a third or a fourth of the life in them. But now the wrath of God is not watered down. The full fury of God's wrath is unleashed upon His enemies, and "every living thing in the sea" is killed. In the earlier chapters, there has been restraint. Here, God is holding back no longer. With these seven plagues, the wrath of God is complete. Beyond just the judgment on Rome back then, the day comes when human government is totally eliminated, to make way for the reign of the King of eternity.

There is also further evidence here in verses 17 and 18 that Armageddon is a symbolic reference to Calvary. I refer to the connection between Jesus' words upon the cross, "It is finished," in John 19:30, and His voice coming again from the throne in Revelation 16:17, "It is done." In both cases, the meaning is that in the cross, God's work of redemption is completed; it is accomplished. In addition, John's vision includes an earthquake in connection with Armageddon in verse 18, reminiscent of the earthquake recorded in Matthew 27:51–54 in the story of the Crucifixion. Though John did not mention this in his gospel, surely he knew about it, since he was there, and makes reference to it here. Clearly, for John, all of history is centered around the Crucifixion, Christ's hill of victory, symbolically referred to here as Armageddon.

Because so much of this chapter is so closely related to the story of the judgment of Egypt, the reaction of the wicked to those plagues is almost predictable. Rather than repent and be spared, even in the midst of their calamity, John says that they curse God still. The followers of the unholy trinity of dragon, beast and false prophet have so hardened their hearts that, like Pharaoh, they do not repent when they see the wrath of God upon them.

There are those today who share the hard-heartedness of the emperor of Rome and his worshipers. They do not believe that there is any wrath of God coming. Psalm 73 describes them very well. They prosper according to this world's idea of success and wealth. They walk in great pride and arrogance. They scoff at the faith of the humble and build themselves up at the expense of others. The faithful suffer much at their hands. They mock God and act as if He is not aware of all that they do and say. They oppress the innocent or neglect the needy as did the power-mad emperors of Rome. They grow rich and powerful and often famous, and receive the admiration and praise of this sinful world. Fools are amused by their sacrilege, when they ridicule the Christian Faith. They do not perceive the end that is in store for them, and they see no need to repent. Instead, as they suffer under God's judgment, they curse and deny Him still. On such, the wrath of God is coming. We do no one any good if we try to deny that part of the Gospel message by saying that a loving God will not destroy the wicked. The Crucifixion is, at the same time, God's ultimate act of grace and the definitive expression of His wrath against our sin. The two are inseparable. The Pastor or the church that forgets this betrays and fails Him.

The seven last plagues John describes are horrible. Yet they are but a token of the wrath that will sweep the wicked away in a moment. All the unrepentant will likewise perish. Pharaoh doubted God's wrath, and it cost his nation dearly. The Romans scoffed at God's wrath, and their empire crumbled before the advance of warriors they considered barbarians. The modern world largely doubts a coming day of judgment, an end of the world, or the fire of hell. But all nations who deny Jesus Christ will go the way of Rome. Only by the grace of God in Jesus Christ are we called to share the Gospel so that more and more people out of every nation of the earth may be spared from the wrath of God. We are not to envy the wicked for their worldly success, nor take delight in their impending doom. We are to take pity on them as they stumble in the darkness, and show them the Light, always remembering that we are sinners even as they are, saved from self-destruction only by the same Christ Who desires to save them. It is our task to lead them to Him, so that they may repent and be saved, for the wrath of God is real. But, thanks be to God, so is His grace through Jesus Christ our Lord.

CHAPTER 12

The Mother of Harlots and the Beast (Revelation 17:1–18)

Anyone who is familiar with the Old Testament prophets is aware that false worship is often referred to by the prophets as fornication or adultery. There is some basis for this in the fact that much pagan worship in ancient times involved ritual prostitution, in which sexual intercourse with temple prostitutes was thought to mimic the union between gods and goddesses to secure continued fertility for the earth by stimulating the gods and goddesses to sexual activity. In this portion of John's account of his vision, he finally explains a bit more clearly what he has on his mind as he describes "the great harlot, with whom the kings of the earth have committed fornication." It is significant that John is carried away into the wilderness to receive this vision of the mother of harlots and the beast on which she rides, for it is reminiscent of Moses, Elijah, John the Baptizer and Jesus, whose great experiences of preparation occurred out in the wilderness.

John refers to the great harlot as "Babylon the great, mother of harlots and of earth's abominations." This is a thinly veiled reference to Rome as being like another Babylon, conquering the world, and spreading false religion as it goes. He makes it even more clear that this great harlot represents Rome in the angel's identification of her as "the great city which has dominion over the kings of the earth." That she is "seated upon many waters" symbolizes Rome's self-serving control of the world government in that day. The city of Rome itself was virtually worshiped as a goddess by the Romans, a goddess representing their own desires and interests. All that was accomplished by the Romans was for the glory of Rome. The empire itself was formed for the benefit of Rome, and John is clearly aware of the attitude of the Romans toward the empire as existing for the benefit of Rome as he writes this book.

Although the earliest emperors of Rome did not like the idea of being worshiped as gods as the Asians wanted to do, they had allowed it to be done, beginning with Augustus, because they knew it would help keep the peace in the province of Asia, and would thus be "for the good of Rome." Later, emperors came to demand that they be worshiped throughout the empire. As a result, what had been intended originally as for the good of Rome, as an accommodation to the Asians, had come to be a threat to the Christians in the empire, as all nations under Rome's dominion had eventually joined the Romans in the false worship required by Caligula, Nero and Domitian.

The beast which has risen from the sea and which has been such an important figure in earlier portions of this book, is seen here again. The beast represents the empire, embodied in each emperor of Rome, culminating in Domitian. Here, John finally tells us of the dual meaning of the seven heads of the beast, which is seen in this portion of the vision carrying the harlot, Rome, on its back. The seven heads represent seven hills. This is simply making it clear that John is talking about Rome and the Roman Empire, for the city of Rome was built upon seven hills. What is a bit more complicated is the designation of the seven heads as seven kings, "five of whom have fallen, one is, the other has not yet come, and when he comes he must remain only a little while." These are the first seven undisputed emperors of Rome: Augustus, Tiberius, Caligula, Claudius, Nero, Vespasian and Titus. When John says that "five have fallen, one is, and the other has not yet come," he is placing the time in which he received the vision as if it were during the reign of Vespasian, the sixth undisputed emperor. It may be only a literary device to give the Apocalypse the flavor of prediction. Or it may be that John actually received the vision during Vespasian's reign and simply did not write it down until he was exiled to Patmos under Domitian. It seems more likely to me that he was already on Patmos when he received the vision. Of course, it could be that he received the vision during Vespasian's reign but did not fully understand it himself until he was exiled under Domitian and, therefore, did not write it down until then. In this case, perhaps the reference in chapter 1, verse 10 refers to an experience of receiving the vision a second time with a new ability to understand it because of his experience. Yet it still seems more likely to me that he received the vision just the one time, on Patmos, and that placing it in the time of Vespasian is only a literary device. That would fit well in an apocalyptic writing.

Concerning Domitian, John says, "As for the beast that was and is not, it is an eighth but it belongs to the seven, and it goes to perdition." In other words, even though it is the eighth emperor who gives John reason to write this book, John is saying that he is not actually a separate emperor, but one of the seven, "who was and is not and is to come." What John is talking about here is that Domitian is Nero, returning for vengeance. There was a well-known, popular superstitious legend among Nero's friends that he would return from the dead to wreak vengeance upon his enemies, which would certainly include Christians. The enemies of Nero were sometimes fearful that it might actually come true. It is said that mothers would bring rowdy children under control by warning them that Nero was going to get them when he returned. John is saying that in Domitian, it has come true, not literally, but symbolically. That is, John did not believe that Nero had literally returned from the dead, but in his estimation, the evil of Domitian and his persecution of the Church was just as bad as if Nero had indeed returned. That is why the mark of the beast, representing Domitian's claim upon everyone who worshiped him, is given as the number 666, which is the numerical value of the name "Nero Caesar," written in Hebrew letters.

Domitian was every bit as evil as Nero had been, and then some. The seventh emperor, of whom John says, "the other has not yet come, and when he comes he must remain only a little while," was Titus, son of Vespasian. He reigned for only about two years before, it is suspected, his brother, Domitian, assassinated him and seized his empire. Domitian, in spite of his obvious evil character, was actually a rather good ruler for the first several years of his reign. It was during the last few years of his life that he apparently lost his mind, believed all that nonsense about him being a god, and added to the murder of his brother all the bloody crimes of persecution against any who did not acknowledge him as "our Lord and our God." Nero had enforced worship of himself as a god, and had persecuted those in Rome who did not comply. But Domitian was extending that persecution, with its murder and torture, into Asia and other parts of the empire.

As for the ten horns of the beast, which represent ten kings who will receive royal power but give it over to the beast, these represent the several nations under the power of Rome. A horn is a symbol of power, and the number 10 is merely a whole number, which represents the whole set of an unspecified number of whatever items are being discussed in a given portion of an apocalyptic writing. So the ten horns represent, not precisely ten of anything, but all the power that the Roman emperor has acquired by subduing all of the kings of the nations which he has forced to submit to his authority.

John tells us in no uncertain terms that by the time of his writing, Rome and the empire had become confirmed enemies of Christ and His church. The great harlot who symbolizes Rome is pictured here as being "drunk with the blood of the saints and the blood of the martyrs of Jesus." How John must have wept as he wrote those words and thought of his brothers and sisters in Christ who had been torn apart by wild beasts in the arena before drunken mobs of blood-crazed Roman citizens or raised upon poles and set on fire to light Nero's garden parties. Rome was truly drunk with the blood of Christ's faithful witnesses. The ten kings are pictured as giving their power to the beast, the emperor who embodies the empire, and together with him, making war on the Lamb, who is Jesus Christ. This refers to how the persecuting madness of Rome under Nero has begun in the province of Asia, under Domitian, the process by which it would eventually spread throughout the empire under later emperors. It is really not hard to see how John could come to think of Domitian, at least figuratively, as Nero coming back with a vengeance. Thus, John paints a very dark picture for the Church, indeed. Their enemy is the beast, the emperor Domitian, absolute ruler of the world as they know it, whose power by virtue of his armies virtually no power on earth could withstand. And he was totally committed to the Church's complete annihilation because those who were faithful refused to call him Lord.

This is but one example of what can happen when godless men become further corrupted by great power. The situation in which Christians in the Roman Empire found themselves during and after the reign of Domitian was very like that of Jews and faithful Christians in Nazi Germany and the nations which were captured as part of Hitler's empire. It was very like the ordeal of Christians in Communist Russia and China in the Twentieth and Twenty-first Centuries, as they have been vigorously persecuted, tortured and executed. There is no earthly hope for God's people when a powerful government, especially one that is dictatorial, sets out to undermine and destroy them. It is something the Church has had to face time and again, in various parts of the world, and in varying degrees of severity and cruelty. Even in this free land of America, the Church is under attack today from certain elements in our government and society who would like to be rid of us.

It is often the case that this kind of persecution results from the adoption by those in power of some alternative religion as opposed to the genuine Christian Faith. In John's day, it was worship of the emperor of Rome. In Hitler's day, it was worship of Hitler and of the German race. When Hitler had them call him "Der Fuehrer," he was consciously taking to himself the title that faithful Christians in Germany refused to give to anyone but Christ. It was the same as when Domitian tried to force Christians to call him Lord. In the Soviet Union and Red China, it has been the worship of man as a worker. In America today, it is simply the worship of mankind or woman and his or her abilities and desires, which we call humanism and feminism. In America and other parts of today's world, there is also the worship of the earth or nature, to the exclusion of the Creator. Blaming humans for "climate change," rather than acknowledging that our planet's climate operates quite independently of us and runs through cycles which we can't influence, is part of the deception coming from this false worship of what God has made, instead of worshiping Him. So is the tendency of some to consider lower species of animals more important than our own offspring, so that animals must be protected while human babies may be sacrificed to Satan through abortion and infanticide. In whatever form it comes, there is that same old marriage of corrupt government and false religion, where the specters of the mother of harlots and of the beast once more arise to trouble God's called and chosen and faithful ones, and to substitute perversion and tyranny, eventually upheld by cruelty, in place of the morality and justice which had once prevailed.

Yet, in the midst of all this gloom that might tempt us to despair, the Holy Spirit provides to us through the words of John a ray of hope. In the vision, the angel says to John, "the ten horns that you saw, they and the beast will hate the harlot. They will make her desolate and naked, and devour her flesh and burn her up with fire, for God has put it into their hearts to carry out His purpose by being of one mind and giving over their royal power to the beast, until the words of God shall be fulfilled." Though it took several centuries for the fall of Rome to be completed, it began the moment a wicked man was given absolute power as emperor and was supported by others, hungry for power. Such a one always opposes God, and such a one always contributes to the ruin of his own domain. That is because, as John tells us, "they will make war on the Lamb, and the Lamb will conquer them, for He is Lord of lords and King of kings." What no power on earth can withstand, He has overcome forever, by His death on the cross and His rising from the tomb. Thus, Domitian, like Caligula and Nero, is long since gone and generally forgotten. Hitler and Stalin and Mao have fallen. Yet the Church they sought to destroy remains. Many Christians have been murdered or tortured or wrongfully imprisoned by those in power who make war on the Lamb by attacking His disciples, but Jesus, Who was Himself also the victim of such men's crimes, has conquered and is alive forevermore. While He lives, the Church remains. No power of evil on earth or in hell can sever us from Him Who has died for our sin and grants us the glory of eternal life. No matter what our enemies, whoever they may be in any age, may do to us, no matter how they make us suffer, those who follow the great harlot and the beast and make war on Christ and His Church, in the end, only destroy themselves. So to us, however we may find ourselves as the Church today besieged by the enemies of the Lord, John's message is, "Be faithful then and believe in the victory of Jesus Christ, even when the present battle seems lost. He has already won the war!"

The Victory of Righteousness (Revelation 18:1–19:21)

In chapter 17, John described Rome, the source of the evils which the Church was about to suffer, as "the great harlot" and "Babylon the great, mother of harlots and of earth's abominations." In chapter 18, he pronounces judgment upon the city of Rome, to which he refers as Babylon, and describes her downfall. He presents a voice from heaven crying out to the Lord's people to come out of Rome so that they will not be corrupted by her evil or caught up in her destruction. He condemns the arrogance of Rome, in which she was so assured of her invincibility. Perhaps remembering the great fire in the days of Nero, he says that Rome is going to be burned with fire under the judgment of God. He seems to have the idea here that the fire in the days of Nero was a warning and a sign of the judgment to come. He tells us that when the end comes for Rome, it will be swift. All the wealth and splendor of Rome, which had taken centuries to build, would be "laid waste" "in one hour." All those who profited by the wealth of Rome or gained power by being her accomplices in her foul and bloody crimes—the kings of the earth, the merchants and the shipmasters—would wail and mourn over the destruction of Rome for the great losses they would suffer by her downfall. But it is significant that they stand "afar off" and lament the passing of Rome. They mourn for Rome only because of what her destruction will cost them. They who shared in her prosperity will abandon her in her time of trouble. Thus the great harlot who has said, "A queen I sit, I am no widow, mourning I shall never see," will find herself utterly desolate and forsaken by all her "lovers" in the day of God's judgment upon her.

At the beginning of chapter 19, the scene of John's vision returns to the heavenly court, and we are presented once more with a spectacle of heavenly worship. It begins with rejoicing over the judgment and destruction of evil, embodied in Rome, in response to the call in the latter portion of chapter 18 to "Rejoice over her, O heaven, O saints and apostles and prophets, for God has given judgment for you against her!" The heavens and the earth and all the saints cry out in answer, "Hallelujah," which literally means, "Praise Yahweh!" God is praised for the destruction of the wicked city because He thus shows Himself to be true and just and faithful to His people. Whenever any such force of evil is brought down, God is to be praised as He is here. For it is by His just power, overruling the affairs of men and nations, that the servants of Satan are defeated and destroyed. Although certainly we must mourn and regret the loss of life that is often involved, we should rejoice that a just God does not allow the evil to prevail forever. Thus, it was fitting that God's people should rejoice at the fall of Assyria and Babylon and Rome and Nazi Germany, even while sorrowing over the wasted lives it took to accomplish their downfall.

In the midst of the jubilation, we are presented a beautiful image of the Church which Christ has redeemed. It is presented as the Bride of the Lamb, adorned not with jewelry or other symbols of material wealth as was the harlot Rome, but simply with the righteous deeds of the saints. This is in stark contrast to the gawdy apparel of the great harlot, who was "arrayed in purple and scarlet, and bedecked with gold and jewels and pearls." As the great harlot symbolized the wicked city of Rome, this Bride clothed in fine linen, bright and pure, who represents the Church, will be further identified in chapter 21 as "the holy city, new Jerusalem." That the Bride of the Lamb is clothed in fine linen which represents the righteous deeds of the saints is not a denial of Paul's doctrine of salvation by grace. We are indeed saved from sin, death and hell only by the grace of God in Jesus Christ, as John would be quick to agree. Yet Paul would also agree with John and James that we are saved not only *from* something, but *for* something. We are saved for a purpose, that we may become righteous and glorify God. The righteous deeds of the saints are the natural result of our salvation. A church with a modest sanctuary, peopled by those who do what Christ would do, is far more beautiful to God than a church that builds a building with majestic architecture and ornate decorations, but whose people just fill space on a pew and do not attempt to do the work of Christ. Simple, active, expressive faith in Christ, producing genuine works of witness and service, is of great beauty to the Lord, Who rejects the artificial glory of man-made and thus false religion. The saints are not just super Christians, either, who are exalted far above the average person. The saints are all who are redeemed and sanctified, that is, all who are made holy, in the blood of the Lamb. Those whom He has made holy produce righteous deeds because of the power of His Spirit present in their lives. The more this is true, the more the Church shares in the glory that is His alone.

An angel speaks to John of salvation as being ultimately an invitation to the marriage supper of the Lamb. It is not surprising that this imagery should be employed in a vision granted to such a devout Jewish Christian as John, the son of Zebedee. Great feasts were such an important aspect of Israel's worship of Yahweh. Jesus Himself had rejoiced in them while He walked the earth. The last thing He had shared with the disciples before His death was a celebration of the Passover feast. It had long been a part of the Jewish expectation of the days of the Messiah that the redemption of Israel would be culminated in a great feast. We should be amazed if John did not think of the coming of Christ in glory in terms of a great heavenly feast. Happy indeed are those who are invited to the marriage supper of the Lamb!

We cannot imagine the splendor of an angel of the Lord. Yet, when John, awestruck, falls down at the angel's feet to worship him, the angel warns him not to do that. As glorious as the angels may be, we are but little lower than they; and they, in spite of their own splendor, recognize themselves as only our fellow servants of God. There was a real temptation to worship angels in John's day, which we cannot quite understand since many people today do not even believe that angels exist. This angel tells John that he must not worship him, quite the opposite of the attitude of Satan, but worship God only. While we may not be tempted to worship angels today, we foolishly worship lesser things than ourselves. How ridiculous and wicked that must be, if we are not even to worship the angels who are so close to God. John comments on the admonition of the angel, saying that, "the testimony of Jesus is the spirit of prophecy." In other words, the affirmation of what we have been taught in Jesus Christ is inspired by the Holy Spirit, Who speaks through God's servants in what they proclaim or prophesy. All the true prophets of God, together with Jesus His only begotten Son, agree that we are to worship none but the one true and living God. If not even angels may be worshiped, how great, therefore, was the sin of those fools who were worshiping the emperor and persecuting those who refused to do so! How great is our sin when we worship wealth or fame or popularity or sex or life itself in the place of God! How great is our sin when we make nationalism or religion a substitute for a genuine relationship with the risen Christ or put the ways of our society ahead of the way of Christ!

Next, John's eyes are blessed with a sight he so desperately longed to see. Being "that disciple whom Jesus loved," how John's heart must have leapt with joy as he recognized in this vision the One Whom he saw seated upon the white horse of victory. Similar to the appearance of Jesus in the first chapter of the Apocalypse, here again, the Lord is presented as One with eyes of flame, which pierce to the very depths of the human heart, and with the sharp sword of the Word of God issuing from His mouth. In the first vision, He was said to be wearing a girdle like that of the temple priests. Here, He wears a robe that is covered with blood, just as the temple priests wore garments made holy by being spattered with the blood of a sacrificial lamb. Of course, in Jesus' case, the blood of sacrifice is His own precious blood. Thus, John presents Jesus to us as the eternal High Priest of our faith, as the writer of Hebrews also does, and as the conquering Messiah.

Here we see Jesus at last coming in power as the great Messiah, Commander of the armies of Yahweh. Yahweh's hosts follow Jesus. They are also on white horses and "arrayed in fine linen, white and pure." This is a symbol of the Church sharing in the victory won by Christ, which is the victory of righteousness. John says that He Who is called Faithful and True "judges and makes war" in righteousness. The warfare that Jesus has won He has waged, not by butchering His enemies, as is the custom of the world, but by being righteous in a world that demands unrighteousness and giving His own life even for His enemies in a world that largely operates on the principle of power and domination. He loved those who hated and spitefully used Him. He was kind to all whom He met, regardless of who they were or what they had done. He perfectly did what was right in the sight of the Father at all times, no matter what it might cost Him, which ultimately cost Him His life. He refused to accept or obtain worldly power by giving in to the temptations of Satan to do things his way instead of God's way. By righteousness which caused Him great pain and self-sacrifice, He gained far more than the mere domination of this world which Satan offered Him. He became King of kings and Lord of lords, Master of a new world yet to come, and the Guardian of eternal life. This great victory and this great treasure of eternal life are to be shared with all who, through faith in Him, are made righteous by sharing in His righteousness. It is a victory won by Christ, not by the slaughter of His enemies, but by His dying for them on the cross.

Dr. Tony Campolo spoke of how Jesus chose to put aside His power while He was on earth and function in terms of love. Dr. Campolo said that power and love cannot both function in the same person at the same time because they are incompatible. He said that power takes over when love fails, and that Jesus came the first time in love; but when He comes again, He will come in power. Yet, I would clarify it is not that Jesus' love has failed, but that the world has failed to respond to His love. Therefore, the world which rejects the righteous love of Christ leaves Him no choice but to return in power. "Blessed are those who are invited to the marriage supper of the Lamb." And you and I had better make certain that we have responded to that invitation and are prepared to be at that marriage supper. For John tells of another feast that will take place also when Jesus comes. He sees an angel standing in the sun. How great must be the splendor of the angels, if one could stand in the sun and still be seen! This angel calls with a loud voice to the "birds that fly in midheaven," which is to say the vultures, "Come, gather, for the great supper of God." We all are faced with the decision of whether we shall accept the invitation to celebrate the feast of the marriage supper of the Lamb, by responding to Jesus in faith and righteous obedience, or instead to be ourselves a part of that other feast at which only the vultures will rejoice.

John now sees the beast and the false prophet, who represent the defiled marriage of false religion and corrupt government in the worship of the Roman emperor, captured and cast into the lake of fire and brimstone (sulfur). Their followers, who revel in the self-made glory of Rome and the empire, come to nothing more than meat for the vultures. Thus all who despise the worship of the one true God, and who make war on Christ and His Church, all who proclaim their own glory and oppress the children of God, will be thrown down with violence, while those who humble themselves and steadfastly follow their Lord Jesus Christ will inherit the glory and victory of His Kingdom forever.

John has presented to us in these words very powerful images of the contrast between evil and righteousness and those who follow each of these ways. The contrast of their final destinies is so great as the contrast between light and darkness, God and Satan, heaven and hell. He is calling us to be faithful to Christ and to live like Him, regardless of what opposition or tribulation we may face, to trust and obey God rather than men, to worship Him alone, and to call no man Lord but Jesus. Those who follow Satan and who trouble the Church may have the upper hand in this world, but their power and their dominion are over a world that is coming to an end. The victory of righteousness imparted to us by Christ is that, even though the rulers of this present world may slay us, when they and this world of theirs are no more, we shall reign with Christ as fellow heirs of a new world that shall be the Kingdom of God without end. Not only that, but the victory of righteousness is also that, trusting in the promises of the risen Lord, we can boldly do the will of our Lord in spite of the threats of the wicked here and now. The greatest freedom we can know is to do what is right while we are under pressure to do what is wrong. This is the freedom and the victory Christ gives, not just for life beyond the grave, but for the daily living of our lives until He comes. Glory be to God Who gives us the victory in Christ Jesus our Lord!

Chapter 14

The Final Judgment
(Revelation 20:1–15)

Through the end of chapter 19, John has been talking about the immediate crisis to be faced by the Asian Christians to whom he is writing, how Satan was at work behind the scenes, making war on the Lord's Church through the emperor cult, how the Church must respond to the persecution they faced, and the judgment by which God would eventually destroy Rome and the emperor cult. Chapter 19 portrays the downfall of Rome as a great victory for Christ which glorifies God. While that chapter finishes the treatment of the subject of Rome specifically, it sets the stage for a representation of events of far wider scope. The reference to the marriage supper of the Lamb points toward the wonderful day of fulfillment that will be seen in the last two chapters of the book. But before those two glorious and beautiful chapters, John must first deal with a subject which is at once dreadful and yet very reassuring.

Having concluded what he has to say about Rome and the immediate circumstances and how they will lead to disaster for the emperor and his worshipers, he now turns to that portion of his vision which has to do with the ultimate destruction of evil in its entirety. In chapter 20, John looks far beyond the fall of Rome to a time yet unknown to us, when not only the servants of Satan, but the great Adversary himself, will be permanently eliminated. The struggle with the forces of Satan in the Roman Empire was but one battle in the ongoing warfare between the people of God and the servants of Satan. In speaking of specific aspects of the persecution under Domitian and how the Lord would deal with him, John has pointed out basic principles of good and evil, the struggle between the two, and the righteousness and faithfulness to which Christ calls us in the face of the world's evil in all ages of history. But here, John begins to speak of the culmination of God's judgment of evil and the great manifestation of holiness that is beyond time, which comes at the end of history.

First, we see an angel of the Lord who binds Satan and casts him into the great abyss of chaos. We are told that Satan is bound "for a thousand years." John says that during that thousand years, those who had been "beheaded for their testimony to Jesus and for the word of God" come to life and reign with Jesus for the thousand years, but that "when the thousand years are ended, Satan will be loosed from his prison and will come out to deceive the nations." Now, this thousand years, often referred to as the "millennium," is the most difficult symbol to interpret of all in this book. There are many different interpretations offered, and there has been much unwarranted division and ill will among some church people on account of the insistence of some upon their particular interpretation as the only one acceptable. Some insist that it means that Christ will return and establish a Kingdom on earth for His saints to enjoy for a thousand years. Others simply try to ignore the reference to the thousand years altogether. Still others offer various other interpretations. No one wants to hear from me or from anyone else that their interpretation is not absolutely correct, but I would say that a lot of the fuss over this is because of so many having some wrong ideas about how to interpret the millennium in a way that accurately reflects what John had in mind here. One thing of which I am certain is that the meaning of this image is not so important in John's understanding as to be worth all the quarreling over it which has at times occurred in the Church, with people on either side condemning the people on the other side as heretics. And I can point out some problems that I see with the interpretations I have mentioned.

First of all, the problem with the main two interpretations, known as the premillennial and the postmillennial views, is that the proponents of both make the mistake of taking the thousand years literally. They fail to recognize that this book is written in symbolic, rather than literal, language. They emphasize the thousand years in a way that is far out of proportion to the attention John gives it. They try to impose upon the text a "historical reality" which its author did not intend to express. By so doing, they deprive themselves of any hope of learning what John was actually talking about, because they thus fail to think through the symbolism of his words at all.

Secondly, this literalism is rather blind to other problems it creates for itself in both extremes. The premillennial view, which states that Christ will return to earth to begin the thousand-year reign, ignores the difficulty of explaining why, if Jesus has returned and established an earthly, literal kingdom, He is not able to keep Satan from escaping his prison and deceiving the nations again. If Jesus came to earth and were established as absolute ruler, it would be unrighteous foolishness or, at least very irresponsible behavior, unbecoming of the Son of God, to let Satan get loose again. The very idea is absurd. The postmillennial view, on the other hand, which states that Christ will return at the end of the thousand years, ignores the violence this does to the text by contradicting the sequence which the text presents and twisting it around to fit the desired interpretation, rather than responsibly following the text itself. These folks need to make up their minds. Do they want to take the text literally or not? If they do (which they shouldn't) I'm sorry, you just can't take the text literally and at the same time change the sequence to suit your own schedule for Christ.

Maybe I can't make up your mind for you about what to do with the thousand-year reign. But I can at least tell you that any interpretation which takes it literally rather than symbolically has no chance of being correct. Both the premillennial and the postmillennial views can be summarily dismissed as irresponsible examples of poor scholarship. The amillennial view, which simply says that there is no millennium at all, but that John has merely reverted to the view of the Judean Zealots, may well have a point, if we assume that John may have lost control of his own writing at this point. But if we assume that John was keeping himself to the use of figurative language, and thus intended the millennium as a symbol of something, then the amillennial view cannot be accepted, either, because it actually shares in the same mistake of taking literally something which John intended to be taken figuratively.

While only the good Lord knows for certain, the most satisfying interpretation I have found is one which recognizes that the number 1,000, which is the cube of the round number 10, symbolizes wholeness or completeness, and not a specific and historically definable period of time. This interpretation says that the thousand-year reign of Jesus and His martyrs represents the permanent victory over Satan that is in effect in every life that is totally committed to the Lordship of Jesus Christ. A thousand years might as well be eternity, compared to the short span of our lives. Indeed, some say that the one thousand years does represent eternity. However, I think it represents a very long time of undefinable limits, and has more to do with a condition than with any specific amount of time. It is a symbol of something complete and permanent. The idea is that Satan is defeated, and there is freedom from his tyranny, wherever the Church or the individual Christian remains faithful to Jesus Christ. That is what this whole book is about in the first place. Wherever the Church or Christian people faithfully witness for the Lord and bear fruit as He commands us to do, Satan is bound and powerless against the Church. That condition is permanent throughout history, wherever the Church maintains its devotion to Christ and its proper influence in the world around it. But wherever a part of the visible Church slackens its devotion and fails to provide the kind of influence it should, then in that place and time, in lives and in societies where the church is not truly being the Church, Satan is unbound because that church has surrendered to him a part of Christ's Kingdom. The letter to Laodicea in chapter 3 warned that the church that they were becoming was such a church. They were becoming "lukewarm" in their commitment and witness, and thus surrendering to Satan that portion of Christ's hard-won Kingdom, which had been committed to their stewardship.

The same thing is true today. As long as a particular church is filled with members who are filled with the Holy Spirit so that they are on fire for the Lord and stand firm in all things as His witnesses, then Satan is bound and helpless before them, and they are experiencing the permanent and complete victory of Christ. But if a day comes when those members of that church who were filled with the Spirit have died out or moved away, and there are left only members of an organization, rather than true members of the living Christ, then that church will surrender to Satan territory Christ has already won from him. The thousand-year reign, that is, as I understand it, the permanent and complete victory, will be at an end in that place, at least for a time. Satan will be "loosed for a little while." And when that happens, a whole community may be lost to an already-defeated enemy. When this is repeated again and again throughout the land, a whole society may be lost to Satan because the churches became "lukewarm" in their devotion and too apathetic to keep the Church alive or to stand up for Jesus. We see this happening all over America and Europe in our day, and it is a dreadful prospect. How tragic it is when a church or a denomination sets Satan free in their area of influence by giving up a battle in the war Christ has already won! John saw it happening in his day, and he wrote to call the Church to wake up and turn back to their original calling and devotion to restore what they were giving away to Satan. May unfaithful churches and individuals learn this lesson and have Christ correct them today!

The rest of this chapter has mainly to do with the final judgment. There are thrones in heaven in John's vision for all the martyrs of Christ, who are granted the special privilege of being raised from the dead already, and not having to wait for the general resurrection. They are granted this privilege so that they might reign with Christ now, as well as share in His Kingdom yet to come. It is only at the end of history, the proper end of the thousand years, that the rest of the dead are raised according to this vision. Since we have already established that the thousand-year reign is symbolic of Christians sharing the completeness of Christ's victory throughout history, it should be clear that John does not literally mean that the martyrs are actually already resurrected and reigning with Christ, or that they will actually be raised at some future date, yet a thousand years prior to the final judgment. Rather, it is a symbolic way of saying that those who take up their cross and follow Christ, those who deny self for the sake of Christ, who lose their lives for His sake and the Gospel's, are living, while they live, in the power of His Resurrection. It is no different than when Paul spoke of our dying and rising with Christ in Romans 6:1–11, with reference to the symbolism of Baptism. John in no way intends for us literally to believe that there will be two separate resurrections of Christ's disciples. Rather, he is saying that those who willingly suffer, rather than to be disloyal to Christ, have attained the freedom from sin and self-centeredness that comes only with a full realization of the meaning and power of Christ's death and Resurrection. He doesn't necessarily mean only those who actually suffer physical death for Christ. Anyone who sacrifices himself for Christ by putting Christ ahead of lesser considerations, anyone who is able to give up personal dreams, ambitions, convenience, or whatever, up to and including life itself, for Christ, has died, figuratively speaking, to any other loyalty that would compromise his loyalty to Christ, and has been raised to "walk in newness of life" (Romans 6:4, Colossians 2:12). Such a person is living in the power of Christ's Resurrection, which is the first resurrection, free to do God's will, whatever it costs, no longer shackled by earthly fears that hindered obedience before. This is the "first resurrection," the raising of sinners above themselves to walk in partnership with God in the here and now by the power of the faith created in us by our risen Lord.

There are some Christians who are weak and unable to bring themselves to risk anything for Christ. They may have a future hope of the coming of God's Kingdom, but they are missing out on the blessings of living this life, day by day, in the power of the risen Christ. But those who are bold witnesses and servants of Christ, doing His bidding and declaring His truth regardless of the cost, are princes and princesses of Christ's Kingdom here and now, as in their lives, God's will is done in earth as it is in heaven. They are martyrs because, as Christ predicted, anyone who does the will of God in this world will suffer as He did. But they are able to carry on in spite of suffering because they have such intimate acquaintance with Christ, and firm confidence in His triumph, that they are open channels for God's action in the world now. Those who have a more timid faith have to wait until the actual resurrection (the "second resurrection" we might say) before they will fully experience such a thorough permeation of their lives by the will of God being done in and through them.

The martyrs are pictured as being seated upon thrones of judgment. The lives of these faithful witnesses, lives lived and sacrificed for Christ, in and of themselves bear judgment upon the wicked and the unfaithful, including especially Satan, the master of faithlessness. This is reminiscent of Paul's statement that "we shall judge angels" (I Corinthians 6:3).

In verses 7–10, "Gog and Magog" is the use of one of Israel's ancient enemies as their representation of all the forces of evil, as was done in earlier apocalyptic writings. Of course, in John's day, the forces of evil were epitomized by the Romans and non-Christian Jews and the emperor cult. These forces of evil, as the army of Satan, are pictured surrounding the Church, which John calls "the camp of the saints," and Jerusalem, "the beloved city." Christian though he may be, John was still a Jew and still held Jerusalem dear, as did his Lord Who wept for her. Even in our day, among gentile Christians, Jerusalem is viewed with a special reverence as the place where our Lord died and rose again and where the Church began. The imagery of the forces of evil surrounding the camp of the saints and the beloved city is not limited to the Romans or to any particular group. John is saying that throughout this world and throughout history, the Church is and will be surrounded by the wicked who are deceived by Satan and seeking to destroy the Church. We shall always have to face them and decide whether to confront their evil with the claims of Christ or appease them as some in the Asian churches and many in the modern Church have advocated. We cannot overcome them in our own strength. But John assures us that God will intervene on our behalf. They will not escape His judgment or the fire of His wrath. We are to keep our eyes on the prize of God's Kingdom and hold on until Christ comes again. Many of us may suffer greatly and even die as the result of resisting Satan's various forces that continually lay siege to the Church. But Jesus' command is "Occupy until I come" (Luke 19:13). The Church is always under attack by those who reject God's way, sometimes more overtly, sometimes more subtly. John urges us to remain true to our calling, and not to fear those who will join Satan in the unquenchable fire.

As they are gathered for judgment and the appointed day arrives, John sees "a great white throne" upon which the Lord Himself is seated. It is white to symbolize the victory and purity of Christ the Judge. When He takes His place upon that throne, then history, the thousand years, is truly ended, as even earth and sky flee from His presence. This is a symbolic way of saying that His coming to render judgment will be just that sudden and powerful. Earth and sky and time as we know it will vanish, and suddenly, we shall be left with no hiding place before the judgment throne of God. We shall be unable to hide from his judgment unless we are under the blood of Christ. In addition, with earth and sky (and all that is contained in them) eliminated, everyone who has worshiped anything less than God will be forced to admit that the things they worshiped were no gods and that only the true and living God is worthy of praise. All the dead will be raised to stand before that throne. Those who have served Satan will be cast out with him from the presence of God. John speaks of the destruction of the wicked and of Satan as being cast into the "lake of fire and brimstone." The symbolism here is in the reference to the images in the book of Satan's working in the realm of human government, which is represented by references to the sea from which the beast arose and the "many waters" upon which the great harlot was seated. Because Satan attacked the Lord's Church, thus "from the sea," he is consigned to a "lake" of fire. It is poetic justice.

Even if we must take the idea of this lake of fire and sulfur (brimstone) as a symbolic reference here, it needs to be borne in mind that Jesus Himself spoke in quite literal terms about the wicked being destroyed by burning. The word Jesus used which we often find translated "hell" is "Gehenna." This word referred to the valley of the sons of Hinnom, where the garbage of Jerusalem was burned. However much symbolism there may be in comparing the final judgment to a burning garbage dump, or to the ironic idea of a lake of fire, the Bible makes it unavoidably clear that the judgment will come, and that those who are not found in Christ will be destroyed. In some way which cannot be literally described, our God, Who the Bible says "is a consuming fire," will indeed eliminate Satan and all of his followers. The consuming fire may be either positive or negative, according to which way we choose to go. For the faithful, God is a consuming fire Who empowers us for vibrant and energetic service to Him. For the wicked, God is a consuming fire Who will leave them in ashes. Having thus destroyed all the unrepentant workers of iniquity, He will thus also have eliminated death itself by doing away with sin, which is the cause of death. So John says that death itself, and Hades, which is the universalized idea of the grave, will be obliterated in that relentless fire.

People try to deny this final judgment in various ways. But you cannot let the Bible speak for itself and still doubt that the final judgment will be a day of great terror and anguish for those who have rejected or betrayed Jesus Christ and His Church. We had better rediscover the terror of that day and make very sure whose side we are on, Christ or Satan. Shall we be allies of Satan and allow those who do not yet know of Jesus Christ to perish with the Devil because we think the idea of judgment is intolerant, or shall we be on the Lord's side and lead as many as we can to be saved by Christ from the wrath of God by faithful proclamation of the Gospel in word and deed? Those are the alternatives that face us. John says we shall be judged for what we have done. Both "small and great," rich and poor, rulers and peasants, it makes no difference who we are. We shall all stand before the Lord and be judged according to what we have done. Jesus will not ask us on that day what church we attended or what office we held, whether ecclesiastical or public, but rather what we have done with the life and witness that He entrusted to us. It is not what we said we believed during this life, but how we lived out that faith in Jesus that will show whether we belong to Him. We should con-sider whether we are ready for that judgment to be made of us today. It could be today. For we never know when that thousand years will end.

That day of terror for the wicked will be a day of glory for those who genuinely belong to Christ. They shall see the end of death itself, and behold the face of God unafraid! John's words, however symbolic, call us to realize our very real need to have the matter decided here and now. If our names are written in the book of life, we shall stand amazed and rejoice in the final judgment when we hear God commend what we shall have done because of Christ living in us. Our only comfort as we consider the prospect of the final judgment is the greatest hope there could be. It is that our fate is in the hands of the same Heavenly Father Who gave His only Son for us. Surrender your life into His hands, and you need not fear to be judged for what you have done.

CHAPTER 15

The New Jerusalem
(Revelation 21:1–27)

At last, John has completed his account of that part of his vision which warns of the destruction of the wicked, and can turn again to the announcement of more glorious and happy news. After the scenes of fiery purification, in which heaven and earth are consumed in God's wrath upon the enemies of Christ and His Church, John sees "a new heaven and a new earth," which God provides in place of the old creation which has passed away. Of course, this agrees with II Peter 3:7–13. In this new creation of heaven and earth, John makes a point to add that "the sea was no more." As we have seen previously, the sea is symbolic of the realm of human government. Satan has been shown to be at work, manipulating that "sea" to make war against God and His people. So this statement is an affirmation that all principalities and powers will have been put down, so that at last, God alone is King. There are no longer any rivals or pretenders to His throne, and thus no more danger to His chosen people, in the new world which will succeed this one. There is also the fact that the Jews were not known for being a great seafaring people, so even that natural danger which they feared will no longer threaten anyone.

The next thing John sees is "the holy city, new Jerusalem, coming down out of heaven from God, prepared as a bride adorned for her husband." This holy city is a symbol for the Church, the Bride of the Lamb. A great voice is heard proclaiming that "the dwelling of God is with men." We are reminded that Jerusalem was acclaimed in the Old Testament as the place where Yahweh God had chosen for His name to dwell. Jesus had promised that God would abide with those who placed their faith in Him. Truly, the Church is the new Jerusalem. The Church is that body of believers in whom God dwells by the presence of the Holy Spirit. It is not yet perfect by any means. But this vision gives us hope. It gives us the hope of a day when we shall receive the blessing of fellowship with God that is unlimited and unmarred by our sin or the troubles that distract us and cause us to wander from Him in this world. There will be no more room for sorrow, fear or pain, for the glory of God will be revealed, and His glory will fill all things, so that everything evil, corrupt, or harmful will be crowded out by the glory of God.

Then John hears the Lord declare, "Behold, I make all things new." There is to be not only a new heaven and earth, but a totally new creation. We who are redeemed shall be new people. I believe the crippled will be made firm and straight. Those weakened by disease or injury or age will receive an irreversible blessing of health and wholeness and the return of the strength of their youth. We shall also be new creatures in that we shall no longer be the prey of temptation, but shall with renewed hearts and minds praise and serve our Creator for eternity. This is the promise of the fulfillment of the new creation Christ began during His earthly ministry.

The Lord further promises, "It is done! I am the Alpha and the Omega, the beginning and the end." This is to say that the matter is settled. He has redeemed His chosen ones and will give them the blessings of His Kingdom, that they might be His heirs and drink "water without price from the fountain of the water of life." No one can change or diminish what He has accomplished, for it is the Lord of Hosts, the Mighty One of Israel, the Master of all creation who decrees, "It is done!" It is the promise of the fulfillment of our purpose. He is the beginning. This not only means that He was there in the beginning, but also that He is the Source of our being and of the existence of all else that does exist. We come from Him and could not exist apart from His will to create us. He is the end. This not only means that He will still be God when all else has passed away, but also that He is our end in the sense of our purpose and our goal. To show forth His glory and be in fellowship with Him is the very reason we exist. That is the end toward which He has created us to be the means. We are not just a great cosmic accident. The promise John shares with us here is that in Jesus Christ, our purpose, our goal, our end will be fulfilled. We come from God, and through Christ, we are going to God. We were created by God for God. On our own, we fall short of our purpose; we stray out of line with our goal. In Christ, we come to the end toward which we were created. Our purpose of glorifying God is accomplished, which makes us complete. For our continued empowerment to glorify God as we are meant to do, we depend upon His filling us with the Holy Spirit, which is the meaning of our being allowed to drink of the "fountain of the water of life." When the great fulfillment comes of which John is telling us here, we shall never thirst for God again, being constantly and perfectly filled with His Spirit. The ecstasy of unbroken fellowship with Him will be given to us for eternity.

However, the Lord states clearly that those who reject Him and His Word, not only murderers, fornicators, sorcerers, idolaters and liars, whom we would obviously expect to see on this list, but also those church members who deny Him and are unfaithful because they lack the courage of the Holy Spirit to be His true witnesses even in the face of persecution, will have no place in His Kingdom. We must remember that John is writing to Christians who face persecution if they refuse to take part in the worship of the emperor. What they were required to do was to go to a pagan temple of the emperor cult, take a pinch of incense, and throw it in the fire on the altar and declare, "Caesar is Lord!" Now that may not sound like much, and there were those in the churches who were teaching that it was all right to make this political gesture and still call oneself a Christian. But John was warning the Asian Christians (and the same is true for all of us, no matter what compromise with evil the world demands) that this could not be accepted. They must decide one way or the other. Either Jesus was their Lord, or Domitian was their Lord. It was as serious as that. If they called Domitian their Lord, John insisted that they had no part in Christ. They would die the second death, from which there is no resurrection. They would be consumed in God's wrath, never to know the joy and glory of His holy Kingdom, never to live again. At issue here was something that had been a deep concern for Israel earlier in their history, as their life before God had been corrupted by the worship of the false gods of Solomon's wives in the holy city of Jerusalem and similar practices by later kings of Judah. As a Jewish Christian, it was deeply distressing for John to see that in his time, Christians were considering making similar compromises. Seeing how taking such a course had led to the downfall of his ancestral people, John was urging upon the Church that those kind of compromises must be avoided at all cost.

The description of the new Jerusalem is patterned after the actual layout of the Old Testament Jerusalem. This is to symbolize the emphasis upon the New Covenant as the fulfillment of the Old. The New Testament Church is the continuation of the Old Testament Church, and its completion. It is the new Israel, which is well symbolized by this vision of the new Jerusalem. The idea is not that God had to change His plans altogether, but rather that the Church as the New Israel is the fulfillment of all that Old Testament Israel was meant to be. Whereas God was not perfectly worshiped and served in the old Jerusalem, where He had caused His name to dwell, He shall be perfectly glorified and obeyed in the new Jerusalem in which "the dwelling of God is with men, and He shall be their God, and they shall be his people." This perfect relationship to God is not presented with any pretense of being the present reality, but rather as the future hope toward which the faithful are moving by God's divine guidance.

Just as in the old Jerusalem, there were three gates in each of the four walls of the city, representing the twelve tribes and thus the twelve Patriarchs, even so this new Jerusalem bears that same mark of the chosen people of God. It also rests upon twelve foundations which bear the names of the twelve Apostles of Jesus Christ. We are told that the walls are 144 cubits in breadth. The number 144, which is of course the basis for the 144,000 we have seen earlier in this book, is a very important symbol. It is the square of the Church number, 12, which is based on the twelve Patriarchs and the twelve Apostles. Wherever the number 144 is used, then, it reminds us that the whole people of God that shall be redeemed consists of all the faithful of ancient Israel, together with all the faithful of the New Testament Church. The dimensions of the city are described as a perfect cube. The cube was a symbol of perfection, being considered the perfect form. All of these images taken together present to us a picture of the wholeness, the completeness, the perfection and the unity of the chosen people of God, Old Testament Israel and New Testament Church, made one in Jesus Christ.

As John seeks to describe this new Jerusalem to us in terms of precious gems, gates of pearl and streets of gold, there are probably treasures of meaning in these symbols which are lost to us today. It is significant that the jewels listed here are the same as those mentioned in Exodus 28:17–21 to be used in decorating the breastplate of the high priest. They are not in the same order, which probably has to do with the fact that God is making all things new, but not without a direct relationship to His original covenant people who were called to be a nation of priests to serve Him. What we can understand is this, that John is trying to describe what defies description. He was attempting to convey to us as best he could something of wonder and beauty and glory that was beyond his ability fully to explain. I think that the best sense we can make out of this is not a literal description, but rather a realization that no matter how beautiful and glorious we may imagine that it will be when the dwelling of God is with men, it will be far greater still. The glory of God that will be revealed to us is far beyond any idea of heaven that we may now possess, and John was merely trying to give us an idea of it in the only terms he could manage. Since the new Jerusalem he is describing is a symbolic representation of the redeemed Church, it is important for us to remember, anyway, that he is not actually describing a literal city or place, but a relationship, since the Church is not a city but a people. Many Christians have believed we are going to "go to heaven" in some way, and that it will be a literal city in the clouds, with streets of gold and pearly gates. This idea is based upon a literalistic misunderstanding of this particular passage, at which John would probably have shaken his head in amazement that we would so misconstrue what he was really saying. What John is saying is not that we shall go to heaven, but rather that God will come to us. The ornate decorations of the new Jerusalem in this vision are merely symbols of the beauty of the relationship with God enjoyed by His faithful ones. The lives of faithful devotion of God's saints adorn the holy city, the Church, the Bride of the Lamb, as she is presented to her husband, Jesus.

It is remarkable that in John's vision of the new Jerusalem, there is no temple. This is something that we could not anticipate a good Jew like John even to imagine. The temple in Jerusalem was just too important even to Christian Jews of the first century for this to be a natural assumption, without a deeper understanding of the theology of the Apostles. It had to be an idea that John received by direct revelation from Him Whose perspective is far greater. It makes sense, however, when we realize the purpose of the temples and synagogues and church buildings that we have in this world. We can't see God here and now, so these structures exist because in our present situation, we need a focal point. We need some place to gather as God's people, some particular place that is set aside and made holy for our gathering to worship Him. In that day, however, we shall have no need for any such special place of worship. We shall be in direct fellowship with God at all times in every part of His eternal Kingdom. There is also the more important fact that the temple in Old Jerusalem was a place where daily sacrifices occurred, seeking atonement for sin. For this reason, especially, there is no more need for the temple, because with the death of Jesus on the cross, all such sacrifices are rendered obsolete.

John tells us that there will be no sun or moon or any other source of light because we shall have no need of them. The glory of God and of the Lamb, which is thought of as a light that shines forth from the very presence of the Holy One, will be the only light, and it will leave no room for any darkness. Emphasizing the glory of God that will fill all things, John also says that the kings of the earth and all nations will surrender their glory to God. This is important. It means the removal of human pride, which is the source of sin. Although there have been some good kings, such as David, the man after God's own heart, and Solomon, who sought only to be a wise servant of God and His people, all kings, including these two, have sooner or later, in some way or other, sought to glorify themselves. David built himself a great palace, and Solomon surrounded himself with great wealth and many women, even bringing the worship of their false gods into God's holy city. Kings are the prime example of mankind's self-glorification. But John says that even the kings of all nations of the earth will no longer seek their own glory. They will all give over the pursuit of their own glory to come and glorify God. This is a great source of hope; for, if even kings will turn from their self-seeking ways, we can be assured that all who are redeemed will also turn from their sinfulness and glorify God as we were created to do.

John says that the gates of the city are never shut by day. This is an important image when we think about the purpose of city gates. They were a protection against the enemy. Many people would live outside the city in ancient times. When the enemy came, the people would rush into the city, and the gates would be closed against the approaching danger. John says that the gates will never be closed in that city because there will no longer be any enemy to attack God's people. The gates always being open also symbolizes God's open invitation to fellowship with Him. When John says there will be no night there, we are reminded that the enemies of God are said to love the darkness because it allows them to hide their wicked deeds. Incidentally, this is another connection between The Gospel According to John and The Apocalypse, since Jesus is quoted in John's gospel as making this very point in John 3:19–21. We look forward in confident hope to that time when there will be no enemy to fear and no evil to hide in the heart of anyone, and the presence of God will be our constant light.

John strengthens this image of hope by telling us that "nothing unclean shall enter it, nor anyone who practices abomination or falsehood, but only those who are written in the Lamb's book of life." This means that there will be nothing to trouble the peace of God's Kingdom. Even our own corrupt relationships with other people, our own unrighteous thoughts and motives, which cause so much turmoil within our own lives and disrupt the fellowship of the present Church, will be cleansed from us. We shall leave all envy and strife behind, and dwell in peace and harmony with God and each other as His chosen people, without end. Praise God!

CHAPTER 16

Back to the Garden
(Revelation 22:1–21)

Following the famous rock music festival at Woodstock (when I was in high school), there was a song often heard on the radio which was written in celebration of that event. One statement the song contained was, "We've got to get ourselves back to the garden." I assume the garden to which the song referred was the Garden of Eden. This was an expression of a common desire to build a new world of brotherhood and peace. Whether the writer of the song had any belief in the Bible, I can't say. But he supposedly did recognize in the story of Eden before the fall of man a world in which mankind could enjoy direct fellowship with God and harmony with each other. To that extent, millions throughout history have concurred with that songwriter in the craving to get "back to the garden."

There is, however, something wrong with the wording of the statement in which the songwriter expressed that desire. You see, the problem is, we can't get ourselves back to the garden. No matter how hard we may try, our own effort, our way of doing things on our own, only gets us further and further away from that peace with God and each other that the Garden of Eden represents. It is only by the sovereign will, decision and active grace of God that we may be restored to the joy and peace Adam and Eve once knew in the garden. That is what this chapter is talking about in the first five verses.

There, in the new Jerusalem, John sees "the river of the water of life," which flows "from the throne of God and of the Lamb through the middle of the street of the city." This recalls Jesus' own use of the image of flowing water as a symbol of the Gospel gift of eternal life through the Holy Spirit, who proceeds from the Father and the Son (John 4:14). It also represents the great river that watered the garden in the Genesis account, for, by the side of the river stands the tree of life. John tells us that this tree bears twelve kinds of fruit, "yielding its fruit each month. The leaves of the tree were for the healing of the nations." Again, twelve is the Church number. This is a declaration that the fruit of the tree of life is only for those who belong to Christ. We have seen earlier that the glory of the kings and nations is brought into the holy city. Here, we see that the leaves of the tree of life have healing powers to heal all who come to Christ from among all nations. Israel had failed to accept God's call to be His agent of blessing to the nations. Here, we see that the Church, the new Israel, will at last be led to fulfill that purpose, as it calls the nations to come to the tree of life to be healed. This is a gentle warning that the Church must realize that the blessings God gives us are not to be kept to ourselves as Israel thought to do. The blessings given us in Jesus are not for ourselves alone, but for the healing of the nations. John further informs us that in that place, "there shall no more be anything accursed," but God and the Lamb will be there, and we shall have eternal fellowship with God, face-to-face.

This is nothing less than Eden restored. Mankind was driven out of the Garden of Eden for two reasons. First of all, Eden was a state of perfect, unhindered fellowship with God. Mankind chose to reject God's authority and became enslaved to sin. There could be no fellowship with God for sinners. Therefore, Adam and Eve were thrust out of the garden and lost the intimacy with God that they had known. Second, they were banished from the garden lest they should continue to eat of the tree of life and live forever. This second reason was not so much an expression of judgment, however, as it was an expression of mercy. It was out of His mercy that God would not allow us to live forever in sin. Therefore, eternal life could never be ours as long as sin is a reality of our existence.

So Jesus has come to take away our sin. He gives us access to the "tree of life." John calls us to see how impossible real, fulfilled, abundant life is for us in our sin. Then, in that awareness, he calls us to rejoice in Jesus Christ, Who alone breaks us free of the shackles of sin so that life can be unendingly everything our Creator intended it to be in terms of glorifying and enjoying Him forever. If we have given ourselves to Jesus Christ, sin has no more power over us. Even death is an enemy we need not fear. We are chosen in Him to see our God face-to-face and live. We are chosen in Christ to share in the inheritance of dominion over a new and unending creation to the everlasting glory of God our Father.

In verses 6–7, the vision John has received is verified as the true Word of God. It will not appear so or be truly understood by any who reject the Lordship of Jesus Christ, but to those who know and love Him as Lord and Savior, the same Holy Spirit Who gives the gift of faith will validate what John shares with us in this book as the truth. A blessing accompanies the faithful receiving of this revelation. All who receive and uphold its truth in faith will be upheld by God's Spirit throughout this life and the next. Foundational to that blessedness is the assurance that Jesus Who died to redeem us is coming again to claim us, and has not now forsaken us, regardless of what outward appearances may be. Though suffering may be the mark of our faithfulness to Him, we are blessed if we remember that suffering was the measure of His devotion to us. This is an important aspect of John's message. There is a blessing even in the midst of trouble, sorrow and pain, when we know that suffering for Christ and His truth expresses our unity with Him upon the cross. Since it is the same forces of evil attacking us that sought to destroy Him, our faithful endurance until He comes identifies us as His along the way.

In verses 8–9, there is a repetition of the warning to worship God only. John's vision makes it indisputable that the original recipients must, at all cost, refuse to worship the emperor, even in order to save their lives. We are to be aware that even the angels, as glorious as they may be, are but servants of God together with us. We must worship nothing in heaven or earth, but our Triune God alone. We must acknowledge as Lord only Jesus Christ Who is God in the flesh, and allow nothing to compromise our loyalty to Him. The angel who has shown John this vision proves himself to be a true messenger of God by redirecting John's attention from himself to God. Ministers of the Word in every age would do well to remember and follow the angel's example here. If we catch ourselves seeking our own glory or trying to gain a following for ourselves, rather than simply leading people to acknowledge through their new life in Christ the sovereignty of God, we should sit down and shut up!

Isaiah had found it necessary to seal up his testimony for twenty years, until a more opportune time, when a new king would mount the throne in Jerusalem who would listen to the Word of God. In contrast, John is told not to seal up the words of this prophecy. Even though it seems pointless to speak the Word of God to the powers that be in the world, God's people and those who can be converted must be given the message. They must be helped to bear the struggle. They must be prepared at any moment to receive the Lord who promises to return suddenly and sooner than the world expects. Time is running out for the world, and we have work to do. The Church cannot do its work without a clear word from the Lord. But we can perform our Christian duties with confidence, for He assures us that He is the beginning, or source, of all things, and that all things are moving toward Him and His Kingdom. He is both the origin and the goal of creation. We cannot fail if we faithfully serve Him. Faithfulness is success in His eyes, even if we die in the attempt, fall short of what we had hoped to achieve, and are scorned by those we seek to save. The horror is that the time is rapidly approaching when everyone who has rejected Him will be locked in to the evil they have chosen, with no more chance to escape. This is foreshadowed by the words, "Let the evildoer still do evil, and the filthy still be filthy." The wicked will continue in their wickedness, thinking they have plenty of time, or that no judgment is coming. By not choosing righteousness, by scorning Christ, they cut themselves off from having a choice to do otherwise. This will happen, but we have the duty not to let that be because we failed to bear witness before them of the truth of Christ. The righteous and holy people of God know that the end of this world is assured, and that we must do what good we can while we can. Because this is their motivation, to do the will of God always, they are secured in the righteousness and holiness they have received from Christ, and will not fall from it.

"Those who wash their robes" are the martyrs, the witnesses for Christ who die for their faith, or at least place faithfulness to Christ above their own lives or comforts. John knows that in the coming persecution, the Christians in Asia will suffer much abuse, deprivation, torture, and even death for the sake of Jesus. He says they are blessed, which means happy. It is not that they should be glad simply to suffer, but they will be happy that they have suffered for Christ. Suffering in and of itself is not a cause for joy, but those who suffer rather than deny Christ are promised the joys of His Kingdom. They can even rejoice in the midst of their suffering, not for the sake of suffering itself, but because of their union with Christ for which the world causes them to suffer. Even those who are not actually put to death may relinquish any claim to their own lives for Christ's sake. John remembers and believes the promise of his Master that anyone who gives up his life for Him shall find it. (Matthew 10:39, John 12:25, and others) Jesus' words in this portion of the vision reaffirm that promise. To those who surrender their lives in this world into the Lord's hands, He gives the eternal life of the world to come, which we can begin to know and in which we can rejoice in the experience of it, even in this world now. We can be in fellowship with Him now, and he does not withdraw His fellowship from those who suffer for His glory and share His struggle against evil. How much happier, then, are those who suffer for the name of Christ than those who enjoy great worldly power and luxury without Him! The latter shall not know the love of God in this world, and they shall not share in the life of glory in the world to come. They shall be shut out from the presence of God, shut outside the gates of the new Jerusalem and destroyed, even as Jesus was shut out of the present Jerusalem and crucified. Everyone who loves and practices what is against the Word of God will be excluded from the new Jerusalem, which means they will be excluded from life. Those who delve into the occult or teach the so-called "new morality" are included in John's list of the excluded, along with murderers and idolaters. So if you think biblical standards of personal morality are outdated, you'd better think again. Witchcraft, sex outside of marriage, homosexuality, and other perversions are considered harmless in much popular opinion today, but God's Word makes it clear that those who practice and those who approve of such things will share the same fate as murderers and worshipers of idols.

Verse 17 is a call to repentance. The message of the Holy Spirit, and thus, the message of the Church, the Bride of Christ, in which He lives and works, the message to all who will hear is "Come." Christ does not desire for anyone to be excluded from His Kingdom. He has freely given His life to open the way of repentance and faith unto eternal life for all who will enter. Our task is to bear this message to a world which does not even realize that its great thirst is for God, Who alone, can quench that thirst with the free gift of life in the Holy Spirit. He alone can fill their emptiness. But to claim that gift requires that we come to Christ. He has come to us where we are, but we must be willing to be turned around and taken to where He is. We must come out of the supposed safety of putting ourselves first. We must come out of the false security of worldly riches and power. We must come out of the stronghold of self-will and self-interest. We must come to the openness of Christ to the Father's loving will and to the needs of others. We must become willing to leave behind all claim to life and privilege and pleasure, and accept the life of service after the example of Christ, depending upon Him in all things. The life and privilege and pleasure He gives far outweigh anything we may surrender for Him.

The warning of verses 18–19 is a warning against editors. It is well-known among Bible scholars that virtually none of the books of the Bible have come down to us exactly as they were originally written. Editors along the way have added portions to some Scriptures and changed wording in others for various reasons. John was apparently aware of this. His prohibition against additions to or subtractions from this particular writing is not to be taken as applying to all of the Scriptures necessarily. We have to remember that John was not writing Revelation to be the last book of the Bible. It was a separate work addressed to a specific situation, as was the case with each book which eventually found its way into the biblical canon. John is simply warning that the original form of this particular book must not be violated. It is a special type of literature composed of symbolic language. To tamper with its wording could drastically alter its meaning, which is already presented in such a way as to bewilder the uninitiated. It presents a clear and specific message to the faithful for a time when they desperately needed it. Not all of its images are clear if we do not know how to decipher them, but the ultimate message that we are to believe in Jesus, maintain our loyalty to Him even at the cost of persecution, liberty, or life, and hang on to our hope in His return no matter what, comes through loud and strong. That message is so important that John warns anyone who would alter it to beware, lest they bring upon themselves the plagues described in the book.

John tells us again that Jesus, from Whom he has received this vision for the Church, promises, "Surely, I am coming soon." The word translated "soon" also means "quickly," "without delay," or "suddenly." The emphasis is upon the suddenness or unexpectedness of His return. It does not seem to us that He has come "soon." Yet, He has been infinitely more patient with us than the patience that is required for us to await His coming again. In one of the books of C. S. Lewis' *Chronicles of Narnia*, the great Lion, Aslan, who is Christ in another form, has promised the children that they will see him again soon. When one of them asks him what he means by "soon," Aslan replies, "I call all times soon." What we need to learn about Jesus' second coming is that He works in His own time. We cannot hold Him to ours, or tie Him down to our preferred schedule. As it is often said of Aslan in the *Chronicles of Narnia*, "He is not a tame lion," so we must realize that we cannot tame Jesus, either. Our concern should be whether we are ready for His coming, whenever it might be. Yet, it is a cry of faith, not of despair, which John voices for the Church: "Even so! Come, Lord Jesus!"

John closes this book with a benediction: "The grace of the Lord Jesus be with all the saints. Amen." Indeed, this is our prayer in all the turmoil of life. It is also our hope and confidence. We cannot withstand the tempests of life unless His grace is with us. Yet we have peace in all our trials when we know Him as Savior and Lord Who came to us in grace and mercy in the first place, and Who promises never to leave us or forsake us. It is important that we understand clearly the meaning of the first five verses of this chapter. Its blessing is primarily a matter of the life to come, of course. However, that life begins for us now, in the midst of this life, by the presence of the Holy Spirit in our lives, if we are in Christ. The message and the promise is that, for Christians, our story ends up where it began, back in the garden with God. Even so! Come, Lord Jesus!

CHAPTER 17

"What About the Antichrist?"

Some readers, perhaps, will notice, and maybe even object, that in dealing with the entire text and message of The Revelation of John, I have made no mention of "the Antichrist." There is a very good reason for this. It is that there is no mention of any such thing in all of the Apocalypse. Yet, I feel it is necessary to deal with this subject at this point, simply because so many erroneously interpret the beast in John's vision as being some individual whom they call "the Antichrist," whom they expect to come at some point in our future. There are many people in the church today who think the Bible predicts the coming of such an individual who will establish himself as ruler of the whole world against Christ. Many of these people, probably most of them, equate this so-called "Antichrist" with the beast rising from the sea, with seven heads and ten horns. As I have explained, however, the beast does not refer to some future individual world leader, but to the emperor Domitian. John never refers to him as "the Antichrist," nor ever even uses that word throughout the Apocalypse.

The only places John used the word "Antichrist," indeed, the only places the word appears at all in the whole Bible, are in John's first two letters (I John 2:18, 22; I John 4:3; II John 7). In these passages, John is not promoting the idea of some future individual who is going to come and establish some one-world society as "the Antichrist." Rather, John was actually trying to correct that misconception which unfortunately still persists among many Christians today, in spite of John's attempt to clarify the matter. What John was clearly saying in his letters was that the Apostles never predicted the coming of such an individual. When the Apostles had used the word "antichrist," the people had apparently misunderstood, as many still do today, and thought they were referring to an individual. John, however, seeks in his letters to refute that idea and straighten this out by telling the people that there is no such individual predicted. Rather, he speaks of a "spirit of the antichrist," and says that "many antichrists (plural) have come." There is not one future individual, but rather an ever-present spirit (or attitude) of opposition to Christ that was already being expressed by many people in John's own day. That is the only proper use of the word "antichrist" that John ever used or acknowledged. We are to be aware of and alert to the growing spirit of opposition to Christ that is being expressed today, just as it has been all along, through antagonistic popular opinion and the institutional bias against the Church and the Word of God. We need to counteract the spirit of antichrist by our daily witness and service to the truth and grace of Jesus Christ, rather than waste time specu-lating and preparing to face some future malevolent individual world ruler the Bible doesn't even really predict. We need to realize that there are many people who are antichrist, both within and outside the visible Church. We need to beware of their influence and study God's Word sufficiently to be able to confound their false teachings. There will even be many world leaders, as there have been already, who are antichrist. But none of them is predicted individually in the Bible as being "the Antichrist." Rather, we are warned about them collectively as expressions of the spirit of antichrist, as John says of his own day that "many antichrists have come" (I John 2:18, again plural, not singular). John tells us that the antichrist is anyone who denies that Jesus Christ has come, or is coming in the flesh. (I John 4:2–3; II John 7) Thus, there are even many preachers in today's pulpits who deny the fact of the bodily Resurrection of our Lord, our own coming bodily resurrection, or even the fact that Jesus is fully God in the flesh, and whom John would therefore call antichrists. So would I.

Now, some would say that "the Antichrist" is the man of lawlessness which Paul discusses in II Thessalonians 2. However, it is clear that John, in his letters, categorically rejects that use of the word "antichrist." I cannot believe that two men who were both Apostles of the Lord Jesus, writing under the inspiration of the Holy Spirit, would be that deeply contradictory of each other over such an important issue. Paul was not talking about some world-ruling individual any more than John was. When Paul speaks of "the man of lawlessness," he is not speaking of an individual in that case any more than he was speaking of an individual when in I Corinthians 1:20, he asked "Where is the wise man? Where is the scribe? Where is the debater of this age?" On the contrary, he is not speaking of an individual, but rather of a type of person which may be represented by many individuals.

What Paul was talking about as the man of lawlessness was not one person, but anyone who fits the description he gives of breaking out of the rule of Christ's Spirit to set himself up as a god or to make unwarranted religious claims to fool people into accepting a counterfeit faith. Paul himself makes it clear that he was not predicting someone who would come in our time or later as an individual fulfillment of prophecy. He says, "the mystery of lawlessness is already at work" (II Thessalonians 2:7). There have been numerous examples of this character of the man of lawlessness down through history. At the time Paul wrote II Thessalonians, it was apparently not so overt or bold as it has grown to be as time has passed, for Paul says it was being restrained at that time, though he does not specify how. We can assume that restraint was by the Holy Spirit. Yet he clearly saw it as already present, rather than something that would appear some twenty or more centuries after his day. After all, Paul did not expect there to be anything like twenty more centuries of human history in this world. Neither did John. Indeed, this spirit of lawlessness has been revealed more and more the longer the world has lasted. In our own time, there is no greater manifestation of the man of lawlessness or the spirit of antichrist than the New Age movement. Never has the rejection of the Gospel been more thorough than in this movement of which Shirley McClane is a part, which calls for mere humans to say, "I am God," and which rejects the notions of sin and judgment and the need for salvation and promotes reincarnation as opposed to bodily resurrection. The New Age movement has its own pretended signs and wonders (II Thessalonians 2:9) in the form of "channeling of spirits," "out-of-body experiences," and various "psychic phenomena." These things are clearly expressions of Satanic activity, as Paul warned us would be the mark of the man of lawlessness wherever we find him. (II Thessalonians 2:9)

Those who try to make this passage from Paul a prediction of some coming monster who will rule the world before Christ returns are taking the passage out of context and fall into the very trap of the devil that Paul and John both sought in their letters to help us avoid. That trap is pointless and fruitless speculation about the end of time that distracts its participants from the business at hand of spreading the Gospel of Christ and building His Kingdom on earth as we are called to do. If we look at II Thessalonians 2 in the context of the whole letter as we should, it becomes clear that in discussing the man of lawlessness idea, Paul was saying to his readers, "Here is the situation we face. The rejection of the Gospel is an ever-present problem. It is going to get worse. So don't get caught up with wondering about the future. Get busy with dealing with the situation you're in now, and be careful not to let yourselves be taken in by the deception of whatever man of lawlessness you may encounter along the way."

In conclusion, let me say that while John was talking specifically about the emperor Domitian, and not about some other specific individual whom we are to anticipate, this does not mean that what he says does not apply to anyone else. In discussing Domitian as the beast of the Apocalypse, John does establish certain principles by which we are to be guided, and history keeps repeating itself in more than one individual. Domitian was not, after all, the first or the last madman to claim that he should be given man's loyalty and devotion in place of the one true God, Whom we know in Jesus Christ. Any time another arises who seeks to make us accept him (or her) as lord instead of Christ, the warnings and instructions we receive in the Apocalypse are to be applied in dealing with that one, as well. Any law or rule of man that is contrary to the Word of God and Christ's law of love is lawlessness before God, and is to be rejected by those who are truly His people. During the murderous farce of the plandemic (yes, I meant to spell it that way) of 2020 to 2022, when the governor of North Carolina ordered churches to close, I urged the Elders of the church I was serving at the time to refuse to close our church. They did refuse, and I sent the governor a message, saying, "You are violating the State and US Constitutions. You have no authority over the Church. I will be in my pulpit every Sunday. Come get me if you like." I never heard a peep out of him, and no one got the virus at our church. Some of us got it elsewhere, but not there, and none of us died. The Lord is still capable today of defending His own against those who would threaten His Church, or at least to honor those who are willing to suffer for Him. From October 2011 through December 2022, I served in the North Carolina House of Representatives. I was the only member of the Legislature, thus far, to have gone to jail for saving babies from abortion at an abortion facility. I am thankful for all the lives my wife and I helped to save, regardless of how the laws of man violated the law of God. He has been faithful to bless us and many others who have obeyed God rather than men. After all, Peter, standing with the other Apostles, told the Sanhedrin, "We must obey God rather than men" (Acts 5:29). While we are certainly meant to be responsible and law-abiding citizens, yet whoever there may be among mankind, at any time, who would, by whatever means, seek to force us to obey men rather than God, they are indeed antichrist, and we must refuse. Glory be to God!

Bibliography

Kurtz, Professor Johann Heinrich. *Church History* (in three volumes). 1883.

Palmer, Earl F. *The Communicator's Commentary: 1, 2, and 3 John, Revelation.* Volume 12, 1982.

Endnotes

Chapter 1

[1] cf. Professor Kurtz, *Church History*, vol. 1, p. 47.

Chapter 3

[2] cf. Professor Kurtz, *Church History*, vol. 1, p. 67.

Chapter 4

[3] cf. Earl F. Palmer, *The Communicator's Commentary: 1, 2, 3 John, Revelation*, vol. 12, p. 158.
[4] cf. Earl F. Palmer, *The Communicator's Commentary: 1, 2, 3 John, Revelation*, vol. 12, pp. 158–159.

About the Author

Larry G. Pittman is a Presbyterian minister in the Evangelical Presbyterian Church. He was ordained on March 20, 1983, in the Presbyterian Church in the United States, and has served several churches, beginning during his time in seminary prior to ordination, having preached his first sermon at the age of eighteen, and having preached at a number of churches during his college and seminary years. He was born in Kinston, North Carolina, on September 30, 1954; was raised in New Bern, North Carolina; and graduated from New Bern High School in 1972. He earned an Associate in Science degree in 1974 from Mount Olive Junior College, a Bachelor of Arts in English with a minor in Religion from Atlantic Christian College in 1976, and the degree of Master of Divinity with Languages from Southeastern Baptist Theological Seminary in 1981.

Larry and his wife, Tammy, were married on August 29, 1976. They raised a daughter and two sons, one now deceased, and they have seven grandchildren. Larry served from October 10, 2011 through December 31, 2022 as a member of the North Carolina House of Representatives. Tammy served as his Legislative Assistant during that time.